The Canadian Address Book

Who's Where and How to Reach Them

ZICKY HAMMUD

Macmillan Canada
Toronto

Canadian Cataloguing in Publication Data

Hammud, Zicky, 1958-
The Canadian address book
Includes index
ISBN 0-7715-9030-X

1. Canada—Directories. I. Title.

FC31.H35 1994 971.0025 C93-095489-0
F1004.7.H35 1994

Macmillan Canada wishes to thank the Canada Council and the Ontario Ministry of Culture and Communications for supporting its publishing program.

Cover and text design: Valerie Cooke

Macmillan Canada
A Division of Canada Publishing Corporation
Toronto, Ontario, Canada

1 2 3 4 5 98 97 96 95 94

Printed in Canada

To my mother and father

"Without communication there is no society, whether it be a hive of bees, a troop of boy scouts or a nation."

Graham Spry

Acknowledgments

I am indebted to a great many friends, colleagues and others who provided inestimable support, advice and guidance during the course of preparing this book. Without their considerable help, *The Canadian Address Book* could not have been completed.

An enormous debt of gratitude is owed to Kevin Colenutt, a colleague and visionary, and to Ken Doiron, a very good friend and former classmate, for their many helpful criticisms, suggestions and intellectually stimulating discussions. Their opinions were eagerly sought and proved indispensable.

For their invaluable insights, ideas and numerous contributions special thanks are in order to Beth Brooks, Jean-Marc Carisse, Yvon Dupuis, Esther Hault, Rachel Liberatore, Paul Perreault, Elizabeth Rand, Linda Sweet and many other friends and colleagues from CAC and FMD. My appreciation also to Nadine Blais, who despite her "seriously pregnant" state, typed the revised manuscript and gave generously of her time and energy to help meet stiff deadlines.

To Marcel St. Pierre, whose computer skills were greatly needed and appreciated, goes my sincere gratitude—his technological expertise is unsurpassed.

To the hundreds of individuals and organizations who provided me with the necessary "intelligence," contacts and addresses, I extend my thanks. The Nepean and Ottawa Public Libraries were important sources of information and their reference librarians were most helpful.

I especially want to thank another special friend, Rowena Sams, for her tireless and diligent assistance in researching many of the names and addresses in the book and her undying moral support and encouragement throughout this project. Her commitment was exceptional.

At Macmillan Canada I wish to thank Denise Schon, Jackie Rothstein, Susan Girvan and, in particular, Nicole de Montbrun, who, as my last editor, has been extremely understanding and a real pleasure to work with.

I must also thank Susan Yates, formerly of Global Press, for initially recognizing the merit in publishing such a book and, consequently, forwarding it to its sister company Macmillan Canada.

Finally, I would like to thank my family for the extreme patience they have displayed during the life of this project. Their forbearance has been remarkable. Thank you all.

Preface

Canadians have been fascinated and intrigued by the notable and legendary personalities of other countries, especially those of our big neighbour to the south. We often fail to realize, however, that some of the world's most distinguished and celebrated citizens are Canadians. Some of them might even live nearby! We have recently celebrated our 125th anniversary as a nation, and I felt it was time that a comprehensive and easy-to-use guide be made available that provides the most up-to-date addresses of some of Canada's better-known (and sometimes hard to find) residents. That is why I've written *The Canadian Address Book.*

With the help of numerous friends and colleagues, I have collected the names and addresses of more than 2,000 persons and organizations who have made a contribution to Canada and, in many cases, to the world. Many of them are household names. Others, while lesser known, have made their presence felt in distinct ways. The only non-Canadian in the book is James Cross, who was the first victim of a political kidnapping in Canada. The names I have included are representative of all segments of society—entertainment, sports, literature, business, politics, art, education, and many other areas. Together, the majority have contributed to the richness and diversity that characterize Canada. However, there are also a handful of Canadians listed who might be considered this country's most notorious and, even, despised residents.

For obvious reasons, I was unable to include in a book of this size everyone who is of note. The intent was to gather together the names and addresses of Canada's best-known and most recognizable individuals (a few of whom preferred not to be included) and organizations without producing the equivalent of a big-city telephone directory. Otherwise, one of the other purposes behind this book would have been defeated, namely, to act as a quick reference guide that is within everybody's reach.

The principal aim of this book is to allow users an easy means to correspond with the individuals listed. Many of us are prevented from writing to well-known Canadians simply because we do not know where to send the letters or how to go about finding their addresses. In my own work as a government consultant and in the pursuit of my diverse interests and hobbies, I have experienced first-hand the frustration of trying to locate accurate mailing addresses. *The Canadian Address Book* is designed to eliminate this frustration.

Despite the difficulties I have sometimes encountered in finding the address of a prominent person with whom I wanted to correspond, whether to ask for some information or just to send a typical fan letter, there is nothing to compare to the satisfaction and excitement that receiving a thoughtful reply can bring.

My experience has taught me that by using the mail skillfully, anyone can obtain the insights, opinions, comments, and autographs of people whom they find interesting or noteworthy. Also worth remembering is that while many of these would-be correspondents are often too busy, or do not want, to take phone calls, they will read and reply to a well-written letter. A letter is never seen as an interruption.

Given advances in technology and the ever-increasing pace of modern life, one would expect letter writing to lose some of its appeal. Indeed, some futurists predict that modern "wonders" such as the modem, electronic mail, the fax machine, and teleconferencing will relegate the art of letter writing to the postal archives.

Despite such dire predictions, instantaneous modes of communication can never provide the anticipation of receiving a long-awaited letter in the mail and the delight that its contents may bring. Canadians love their mail. According to Canada Post, each Canadian receives, on average, more than 350 pieces of mail every year.

Although postal-rate increases have become somewhat of an annoying annual event, the cost of mailing a letter in Canada continues to be a bargain. For under fifty cents, one can still mail a first-class letter to or from anywhere in Canada, across six time zones from the Atlantic to the Pacific to the Arctic. Considering the enormous effect that a well-written letter has on its recipient, the cost of a postage stamp is truly negligible.

Whether one corresponds to request specific information from a scholar, seek the autograph of a rock idol or sports hero, challenge a politician, or just for the simple pleasure of writing, letter writing truly is an individual art form. As Rosemary Sullivan so masterfully explained in her review (*The Globe and Mail*, May 29, 1993) of John Lennox's book, *Margaret Laurence–Al Purdy: A Friendship in Letters: Selected Correspondence*, "Letters are ephemeral documents. We write them at the end of the day, out of momentary enthusiasms or depressions, inventing ourselves for the person who is to receive them." This is only one of the many eloquent tributes paid to letter writing over the years. They themselves possess a certain beauty, and so I have decided to include some of them at the beginning of each section of this book. I am sure you will enjoy them as much as I do.

A FEW WORDS ON ETIQUETTE

The pages that follow will, I hope, propel you to write to some of the people listed. Who knows, it might even lead to a regular correspondence. As with any form of communication, there is a proper etiquette to be observed when writing a letter. Here are some rules to remember.

Always enclose a self-addressed stamped envelope (SASE).

Notable people receive a lot of mail. To help ensure that you receive a reply, be considerate and enclose a SASE. Remember, although people may be well known, this does not mean that they can afford the postage required to reply to hundreds or thousands of letters. A letter that includes a SASE will most likely be given priority over those that do not.

Begin every letter by introducing yourself and explain briefly why you are writing.

Always use clear and concise language. Since most of the people listed in this collection are very busy, letters should be kept brief; otherwise, they may not be read immediately. Do not ramble on.

Write legibly.

Nothing is more frustrating than receiving a hand-written letter that is unreadable. If you do not have access to a typewriter or word processor, try to write slowly and neatly. If your handwriting is very bad, try printing. The visual quality of a letter will often invite the recipient to read the letter and to take it more seriously.

Be courteous and get to the point.

Whether you are writing a letter of complaint to an executive or a letter of criticism to a politician, you will always be more successful if you write in a polite and reasonable manner. In some cases (for example, when writing to the more infamous Canadians listed in this book), this might be more difficult to do but try, nonetheless. Hostile or overly emotional letters will, more often than not, be dismissed by the recipient as irrational and unsophisticated.

If requesting something, always thank the individual in advance and don't forget to include your return address in the letter.

Don't assume that the person you are writing to is obligated to fulfill your request; express your appreciation in advance. Many people fail to receive replies to their letters simply because they failed to include a return address.

Ensure that the address on the envelope is correct and sufficient postage is affixed.

Many letters are returned to the sender because of an incorrect address or insufficient postage. Speaking of postage (and being a stamp collector myself), consider using attractive or interesting stamps on your envelopes. Canada Post issues approximately fifty stamps each year commemorating various events and figures. They do not cost any more than regular-issue stamps but add a special touch. The recipient might even be a stamp collector!

While I have endeavoured to include the most up-to-date addresses I could find, I cannot guarantee that these will not change. Like all Canadians, many of the people in this book are highly mobile and therefore change addresses frequently. In such cases, letters are usually forwarded to them from their last address. This is not always the case; sometimes letters are returned to the sender. If you know that an individual is no longer at the address listed in this book, the best way to locate the new address is to contact the organization with which that person was previously associated.

If you have made a name for yourself in a particular area or know of someone who has, please send any relevant information along for possible inclusion in a future edition of this book. Similarly, if you would like to share any interesting or unusual correspondences you have had as a result of the information in *The Canadian Address Book*, I would love to hear from you. Please remember to include a SASE if you would like to hear back from me. I look forward to receiving your letters. Send any correspondence to:

Zicky Hammud
P.O. Box 55128
240 Sparks St. Stn.
Ottawa, ON K1P 1A1

Now that you have *The Canadian Address Book*, why not write that letter you've been putting off. Don't procrastinate.

A

"The Pen is the Tongue of the Mind."

Cervantes

Aaron, Lee *rock singer*	c/o 1407 Mount Pleasant Rd. Toronto, ON M4N 2T9
Aaron, Raymond *real estate entrepreneur/* *professional speaker*	482 Queen St. Newmarket, ON L3Y 2H4
Abel, Allen J. CBC TV journalist	100 Carlton St. Toronto, ON M5W 1A0
Abella, Irving President, Canadian Jewish Congress *author/professor*	c/o Dept. of History Glendon College 2275 Bayview Ave. Toronto, ON M4N 3M6
Abella, Rosalie Judge, Ontario Court of Appeal/*author*	375 Glengrove Ave. W. Toronto, ON M5N 1W4
***Abilities* magazine** Raymond Cohen, Publisher/Editor *Canada's lifetsyle magazine for* *people with disabilities*	P.O. Box 527, Stn. P Toronto, ON M5S 2T1
Abitibi-Price Inc. Bernd Koken, Chairman and CEO *newsprint maker*	207 Queen's Quay W. Box 102 Toronto, ON M5J 2P5
Acadia University Kelvin K. Ogilvie, President	Wolfville, NS B0P 1X0

Action Canada Network
Tony Clarke,
National Chairman
anti-free trade organization

251 Laurier Ave. W., #904
Ottawa, ON K1P 5J6

Adams, Bryan
rock singer/songwriter

c/o Bruce Allen Talent
68 Water St., Ste. 406
Vancouver, BC V6B 1A4

Adams, Willie
Liberal Senator from the
Northwest Territories

Room 581-F
The Senate
Ottawa, ON K1A 0A4

Adaskin, Murray
"Dean of Canada's Composers"

3020 Devon Rd.
Victoria, BC V8R 6C9

Aga Khan Foundation Canada
Nazeer Aziz Ladhani, CEO
international development agency

Waterpark Place
10 Bay St., Ste. 610
Toronto, ON M5J 2R8

Aglukark, Susan
the "Arctic Rose" Inuit singer/activist

201 Florence St.
Ottawa, ON K1R 5N5

AGT
Donald J. Lowry, President
Alberta telephone company

10020 100 St.
Edmonton, AB T5J 0N5

Air Atlantic Ltd.
Neal Jackman, President

1888 Brunswick St., #803
Halifax, NS B3J 3J8

Air BC
Iain Harris, President

4740 Agar Dr.
Richmond, BC V7B 1A6

Air Canada
Hollis Harris, CEO

Air Canada Place
Montreal, PQ H2Z 1X5

Air Nova
Joe Randell, President and CEO

1550 Bedford Hwy., Ste 500
Bedford, NS B4A 1E6

Air Ontario Inc.
Roger W. Linder, Chairman

Air Ontario Drive
London, ON N5V 3S4

Aislin
(Terry Mosher)
editorial cartoonist

c/o *The Gazette*
250 rue St-Antoine ouest
Montreal, PQ H2Y 3R7

Alanis
(Alanis Morissette)
rock singer
1700 Broadway
New York, NY 10019
U.S.A.

Alberta Stock Exchange
Thomas A. Cumming,
President and CEO
300 5th Ave., 21st fl.
Calgary, AB T2P 3C4

Alcan Aluminium Ltd.
Jacques Bougie,
President and CEO
1188 Sherbrooke St. W.
Montreal, PQ H3A 3G2

Alcoholics Anonymous (AA)
S.A. Steinman,
Executive Director
#502, 234 Eglinton Ave. E.
Toronto, ON M4P 1K5

Alexander, Lincoln MacCauley
former Lieutenant-Governor
of Ontario
30 Proctor Blvd.
Hamilton, ON L8M 2M3

Alexander Graham Bell Museum
John W. Stephens,
Superintendent
P.O. Box 159
Baddeck, NS B0E 1B0

Allaire, Jean
Leader, Groupe Action-Québec
7715 rue Papineau, Ste. 103
Montreal, PQ H2E 2H4

Allen, Charlotte Vale
(Katherine Marlowe)
author
144 Rowayton Woods Dr.
Norwalk, Conn. 06854
U.S.A.

Alliance for a Drug Free Canada
Jacques Perras, Director
#800, 180 Elgin St.
Ottawa, ON K2P 2K3

Alliance for the Preservation of English in Canada (APEC)
Ronald P. Leitch, President
supports unity through one official language
#5068, 3080 Yonge St.
Toronto, ON M4N 3N1

Alliance of Canadian Cinema, Television and Radio Artists (ACTRA)
Alexander Crawley, President
2239 Yonge St.
Toronto, ON M4S 2B5

Alliance Quebec
Robert J. Keaton, President
fosters the preservation of the English language in Quebec

980 rue St-Antoine ouest
Ste. 310
Montreal, PQ H3C 1A8

Allmand, Warren
Liberal MP from Quebec/former Cabinet Minister

Room 104-EB
House of Commons
Ottawa, ON K1A 0A6

Alta Moda
rock band

c/o Current
366 Adelaide St. E.
Ste. 437
Toronto, ON M5A 3X9

Alzheimer Society of Canada
Stephen Rudin,
Executive Director

#201, 1320 Yonge St.
Toronto, ON M4T 1X2

Amagoalik, John
Inuit leader/"Father of Nunavut"

130 Slater St., Ste. 800
Ottawa, ON K1P 6E2

American Barrick Resources Corporation
Peter Munk, Chairman and CEO
gold mining company

24 Hazelton Ave.
Toronto, ON M5R 2E2

American Express Canada Inc.
Alan Stark, President

101 McNabb St.
Markham, ON L3R 4H8

Amiel, Barbara
journalist

c/o *The Toronto Sun*
333 King St. E.
Toronto, ON M5A 1A1

Amnesty International
(Canadian Section/
English Speaking)
Roger Clark, Secretary General

#900, 130 Slater St.
Ottawa, ON K1P 6E2

Amnistie Internationale
(Canadian Section/
French Speaking)
Gilles Corbeil, Directeur General

3516 av. du Parc
Montreal, PQ H2H 2H7

Anderson, David
federal Liberal Cabinet Minister from B.C./former provincial Party Leader

Room 133-EB
House of Commons

Anderson, Doris *writer/women's activist*	c/o The Writers' Union of Canada 24 Ryerson Ave. Toronto, ON M5T 2P3
Anderson, John R., Admiral Ambassador to NATO/former Chief of the Defence Staff	Delegation of Canada Léopold III Blvd. 1110 Brussels, Belgium
Andre, Harvie former federal Conservative Cabinet Minister	c/o Suncor Inc. Board of Directors 36 York Mills Rd. North York, ON M2P 2C5
Andres Wines Ltd. Joseph A. Peller, Chairman, CEO and President	P.O. Box 550 Winona, ON L0R 2L0
Andrew, HRH The Prince The Duke of York	Buckingham Palace London SW1, England
Andreychuk, Raynell Conservative Senator from Saskatchewan	Room 589-S The Senate Ottawa, ON K1A 0A4
Angonactuaq, Elizabeth *artist*	Baker Lake, NT X0C 0A0
Angus, David W. Conservative Senator	Room 808-VB The Senate Ottawa, ON K1A 0A4
Animal Defence League of Canada J. Belair, Manager	P.O. Box 3880, Stn. C Ottawa, ON K1Y 4M5
Anka, Paul *pop singer*	P.O. Box 100 Carmel, CA 93921 U.S.A.
Anne, HRH The Princess	Gatcombe Park Gloucestershire, England
Anne of Green Gables Museum	c/o Kindred Spirits Avonlea, PE C0B 1M0
Anne Murray Centre Shelagh Rayworth, Executive Director	P.O. Box 610 Springhill, NS B0M 1X0

Appel, Bluma
philanthropist
18A Hazelton Ave., Apt. 405
Toronto, ON M5R 2E2

Apple Canada, Inc.
Peter V. Jones, President
7495 Birchmount Rd.
Markham, ON L3R 5G2

Applebaum, Louis
composer/conductor
c/o Affiliated Arts Co.
1210 Don Mills Rd., #214
Don Mills, ON M3B 3N9

Appleyard, Peter
composer
315 Soudan Ave.
Toronto, ON M4S 1W6

Arcand, Denys
film director/producer
4921 rue Coronet, Ste. 12
Montreal, PQ H3V 1C9

Arcand, Gabriel
founder and director,
Le Groupe de la Veillée
actor
1371 rue Ontario est
Montreal, PQ H2L 1S2

Archambault, Louis
sculptor
278 av. Sanford
St-Lambert, PQ J4P 2X6

Archer, Doug
Mayor of Regina
P.O. Box 1790
Regina, SK S4P 3C8

Archer, Violet B.
composer/pianist
10805 85th Ave.
Edmonton, AB T6E 2L2

***Arctic* magazine**
Karen McCullough, Editor
The University of Calgary
2500 University Dr. N.W.
Calgary, AB T2N 1N4

Arctic Winter Games Corp.
Don Cooper, President
P.O. Box 818
Yellowknife, NT X1A 2N6

Army, Navy, Air Force Veterans in Canada (ANAVETS)
Ian D. Inrig, Dominion Secretary
Canada's oldest veterans' association
6 Beechwood Ave., Ste. 2
Ottawa, ON K1L 8B4

Art Gallery of Ontario (AGO)
Glen Lowry, Director
317 Dundas St. W.
Toronto, ON M5T 1G4

Arthritis Society
John L.M. Clippingdale,
President and CEO
#401, 250 Bloor St. E.
Toronto, ON M4W 3P2

Asper, Israel
Chairman and CEO,
CanWest Global Communications
600 One Lombard Place
Winnipeg, MB R3B 0X3

Asselin, Martial
Lieutenant-Governor of Quebec
Maison de la Gouvernement
1050 rue St-Augustin
Quebec, PQ G1A 1A1

Association for Canadian Studies
Beatrice Kowaliczko,
Executive Director
P.O. Box 8888, Stn. A
Montreal, PQ H3C 3P8

Association of Canadian Ultramarathoners
David Blaikie, President
5515 Millview Rd.
Manotick, ON K4M 1J3

Association of Iroquois and Allied Indians
Harry Doxtator, Grand Chief
R.R. #2
Southwold, ON N0L 2G0

Association of Universities and Colleges of Canada (AUCC)
Claude Lajeunesse, President
350 Albert St., Ste. 600
Ottawa, ON K1R 1B1

Asthma Society of Canada
Elizabeth Kovac,
Executive Director
130 Bridgeland Ave.
Ste. 425
Toronto, ON M6A 1Z4

Athabasca University
Terry Morrison, President
Box 10,000
Athabasca, AL T0G 2R0

Atkins, Norman
Conservative Senator from Ontario
Room 208-EB
The Senate
Ottawa, ON K1A 0A4

Atlantic Federation of Musicians
Peter Power, President
Site 3, Box 5522
R.R. #5
Armdale, NS B3L 4J5

Atlantic Provinces Economic Council (APEC)
Brian Crowley, President
5121 Sackville St., Ste. 500
Halifax, NS B3J 1K1

Atlantis Films Ltd.
Kevin Shea, President and
Chief Operating Officer
TV production company
65 Heward Ave., Ste. 201
Toronto, ON M4M 2T5

Atomic Energy of Canada Ltd. (AECL)
Stanley R. Hatcher,
President and CEO

344 Slater St.
Ottawa, ON K1A 0S4

Atwood, Margaret
author

c/o McClelland & Stewart
481 University Ave.
Ste. 900
Toronto, ON M5G 2E9

Auf der Maur, Nick
municipal politician/journalist

c/o *The Gazette*
250 rue St-Antoine ouest
Montreal, PQ H2Y 3R7

Augustyn, Frank
choreographer/ballet star
Director, Ottawa Ballet

P.O. Box 366, Stn. A
Ottawa, ON K1N 8V3

Austin, Jack
Liberal Senator from B.C.

Room 304-VB
The Senate
Ottawa, ON K1A 0A4

Autism Society Canada
Laurie Turza, Executive Director

129 Yorkville Ave.
Ste. 202
Toronto, ON M5R 1C4

Avon Canada Inc.
Christina Gold,
President and CEO

5500 Trans-Canada Hwy.
Pointe Claire, PQ H94 1B6

Axworthy, Lloyd
Liberal
Federal Cabinet Minister
from Manitoba

Room 420-N
House of Commons
Ottawa, ON K1A 0A6

Axworthy, Thomas Sydney
Executive Director, The CRB Foundation/former adviser to the Prime Minister

1170 Peel St.
Montreal, PQ H3B 4P2

Aykroyd, Dan
actor/comedian

9200 Sunset Blvd., #428
Los Angeles, CA 90069
U.S.A.

Ayre, Miller H.
Chairman and CEO, Ayre's Ltd.

P.O. Box 70
St. John's, NF A1C 5H8

Aziz, Philip
painter/sculptor/designer

1180 Western Rd.
London, ON N6G 1G8

B

"This is a free country. Folks have a right to send me letters, and I have a right not to read them."

William Faulkner

Bachle, Leo (Les Barker) *creator of Canada's first popular comic book hero, "Johnny Canuck" /comedian*	3585 Sheppard Ave. Toronto, ON M1T 3K8
Bachman, Randy *songwriter and guitarist, Bachman-Turner Overdrive (BTO) and The Guess Who*	c/o Bruce Allen Talent 68 Water St., Ste. 406 Vancouver, BC V6B 1A4
Back, Frederic *animation film producer*	Société Radio-Canada 1400 est René-Lévesque Montreal, PQ H2L 2M2
Baha'i Community of Canada M.E. Muttart, General Secretary	7200 Leslie St. Thornhill, ON L3T 6L8
Bailey, Alfred Goldsworthy *author*	2 Acacia Court Fredericton, NB E3B 1Y7
Bain, Conrad *actor*	1901 Avenue of the Stars Los Angeles, CA 90067-6001 U.S.A.
Bain, George *journalist*	R.R. #2 Oakland Mahone Bay, NS B0J 2E0
Baker, Carroll *country singer*	210 Dimson St. Guelph, ON N1G 3C8
Baldry, "Long John" *folk singer*	P.O. Box 861 Edmonton, AB T5J 2L8

Balfour, James
Conservative Senator from Saskatchewan

Room 207-EB
The Senate
Ottawa, ON K1A 0A4

Les Ballets Jazz de Montreal
Caroline Salbaing, General Manager

3450 rue St-Urbain
Montreal, PQ H2X 2N5

The Band
rock group

c/o Fogel-Sabourin Productions
4200 boul. St-Laurent, Ste. 1400
Montreal, PQ H2W 2R2

Bank of Montreal
Matthew Barrett, Chairman
Canada's third-largest bank

Place d'Armes
P.O. Box 6002
Montreal, PQ H2Y 3S8

Bank of Nova Scotia
Peter Godsoe, CEO
Canada's fourth-largest bank

Scotia Plaza
44 King St. W.
Toronto, ON M5H 1H1

Banks, Tommy
pianist/conductor/composer

#2, 12227 107th Ave.
Edmonton, AB T5M 1Y9

Banting Museum and Education Centre
Grant Maltman, Curator
devoted to the achievements of Dr. Frederick Banting, the co-discoverer of insulin

442 Adelaide St. N.
London, ON N6B 3H8

Barbeau, Marcel
abstract painter/sculptor

1635 rue Amherst
Montreal, PQ H2L 3L4

Bare Naked Ladies
rock band

38 Cumberland Lane
Ajax, ON L1S 7K4

Barney Bentall & The Legendary Hearts
rock band

c/o 1505 West 2nd. Ave.
Ste. 200
Vancouver, BC V6H 3Y4

Barris, Alex
TV scriptwriter

6 Malamute Cres.
Agincourt, ON M1T 2C7

Bartklw, Roman
artist

P.O. Box 100
Paradise, NS B0S 1R0

Basketball Canada
Rick Traer, Executive Director

1600 James Naismith Dr.
Gloucester, ON K1B 5N4

Bassett, Carling
tennis star
c/o Tennis Canada
3111 Steeles Ave. W.
Downsview, ON M3J 3H2

Bassett, Douglas
CEO, Baton Broadcasting Inc.
P.O. Box 9, Stn. O
Toronto, ON M4A 2M9

Bastarache, Michel
Acadian leader/insurance company president
c/o Assumption Mutual Life
P.O. Box 160
Moncton, NB E1C 8L1

Bata, Thomas J.
President and CEO, Bata Ltd.
world's largest shoe manufacturer
59 Wynford Dr.
Don Mills, ON M3C 1K3

Bata Shoe Museum Collection
Jonathan Walford, Curator
59 Wynford Dr.
Don Mills, ON M3C 1K3

Bateman, Robert
wildlife artist
Fulford Harbour
Salt Spring Island
BC V0S 1C0

Batten, Jack
author
199 Albany Ave.
Toronto, ON M5R 3C7

Bauer, Steve
cyclist, Olympic medallist
567 Metler Rd.
Ridgeville, ON L0S 1M0

Baumann, Alex
swimmer, Olympic medallist
2617 Field St.
Sudbury, ON P3E 4X8

BCE Inc.
Lynton R. "Red" Wilson,
Chairman and CEO
2000 McGill College Ave.
Ste. 2100
Montreal, PQ H3A 3H7

B.C. Lions Football Club
Eric Tillman, General Manager
808 W. Hastings St.
Vancouver, BC V6C 2X4

Bearskin Airlines
Cliff and Harvey Freisen, owners
1475 West Walsh St.
Thunder Bay, ON P7E 4X6

Beauchemin, Yves
author
247 rue St-Jacques
Longueuil, PQ J4H 3B8

Beaudoin, Gérald-A.
Conservative Senator
from Quebec
Room 474-F
The Senate
Ottawa, ON K1A 0A4

Beaulieu, Mario
Conservative Senator
from Quebec
Room 602-VB
The Senate
Ottawa, ON K1A 0A4

The Beaver
Christopher Dafoe, Editor
Canadian history magazine
450 Portage Ave.
Winnipeg, MB R3C 0E7

Beaverbrook, Lady
(Marcia Dunn)
widow of Lord Beaverbrook
Dayspring
Saint Andrews, NB E0G 2X0

Beaverbrook Art Gallery
Ian G. Lumsden, Director
P.O. Box 605,
Fredericton, NB E3B 5A6

Beck, Nuala
economist/author
BCE Place, 161 Bay St.
P.O. Box 531
Toronto, ON M5J 2S1

Beckman, Henry H.G.
actor
3906 Nelson Rd.
Deming, WA 98244
U.S.A.

Beecroft, Norma Marian
composer
10 Lyndhurst Court
Toronto, ON M5R 1X7

Beigie, Carl
economist
c/o RBC-Dominion Securities
Inc.
200 Bay St., 25th fl.
Toronto, ON M5J 2J2

Bell, John Kim
symphony conductor/founder,
Canadian Native Arts
Foundation
77 Mowat Ave., Ste. 508
Toronto, ON M6K 3E3

Bell, Rev. Linda
Moderator, Presbyterian
Church of Canada
50 Wynford Dr.
ON M3C 1J7
Toronto, ON

Bell, Marilyn
first person to swim across
Lake Ontario (1954)
c/o Canada Sports Hall of Fame
Exhibition Place
Toronto, ON M6K 3C3

Bell Canada
John McLennan
President and CEO
1050 Beaver Hall Hill
Montreal, PQ H2Z 1S4

Belliveau, Jean
former hockey player
155 rue Victoria
Longueuil, PQ J4H 2J4

Belliveau, Véronique
rock singer
137 St-Pierre, Ste. P121
Montreal, PQ H2Y 2L6

Bellow, Saul
Nobel Prize-winning author

c/o Committee on Social Thought
University of Chicago
1126 E. 59th St.
Chicago, IL 60637 U.S.A.

Belzburg, Samuel
financier

1177 W. Hastings St.
Ste. 2000
Vancouver, BC V6E 2K3

Benmergui, Ralph
broadcaster/former TV talk show host

c/o CBC
P.O. Box 500, Stn. A
Toronto, ON M5W 1E6

Bennett, Bill
former Premier of B.C.

R.R. #1, Pritchard Dr.
Westbank, BC V1Y 7P9

Bercuson, David Jay
author/historian

Faculty of Graduate Studies
University of Calgary
2500 University Dr. N.W.
Calgary, AB T2N 1N4

Beresford-Howe, Constance
author

225 Moore Ave.
Toronto, ON M4G 1C6

Berger, Thomas
former Judge,
Supreme Court of B.C.
aboriginal rights defender

#300, 171 Water St.
Vancouver, BC V6B 1A7

Bernardi, Mario
conductor

c/o Calgary Philharmonic Orchestra
205 8th Ave. S.E.
Calgary, AB T2G 0K9

Bernardo (Teale), Paul
charged with schoolgirl murders and numerous sexual assault crimes

c/o Special Needs Unit 2-A
Metro East Detention Centre
55 Civic Rd.
Scarborough, ON M1L 2K9

Berntson, Eric Arthur
Conservative Senator from Saskatchewan

Room 621-VB
The Senate
Ottawa, ON K1A 0A4

Berton, Pierre
author

21 Sackville St.
Toronto, ON M5A 3E1

Bessette, Gérard
author

270 Frontenac St.
Kingston, ON K7L 3S8

Bethune Memorial House and Museum
Maryellen Corcelli,
Chief of Visitor Activities
devoted to the life and work of Dr. Norman Bethune

P.O. Box 2160
Gravenhurst, ON P0C 1G0

Bettman, Gary
first NHL Commissioner

650 Fifth Ave.
New York, NY 10019
U.S.A.

Bey, Salome
singer

c/o Great World Artists Management Inc.
66 Gerrard St. E., Ste. 201
Toronto, ON M5B 1G3

Big Brothers of Canada
Michael Howorth,
National Executive Director

5230 South Service Rd.
Burlington, ON L7L 5K2

Bigelow, Dr. Wilfred Gordon
pacemaker inventor/heart surgeon

7 Castle Frank Rd.
Toronto, ON M4W 2Z3

Billes, Alfred
founder, Canadian Tire

c/o Canadian Tire Corp. Ltd.
P.O. Box 770, Stn. K
Toronto, ON M4P 2V8

Bird, Florence Bayard
former Liberal Senator
women's rights activist

201, 333 Chapel St.
Ottawa, ON K1N 8Y8

Birks, Henry Jonathan
jeweller/President and CEO,
Henry Birks and Sons (1993) Inc.

1240 Phillips Square
Montreal, PQ H3B 3H4

Birney, Earle
author

#1204, 130 Carlton St.
Toronto, ON M5A 4K3

Bishop's University
Hugh Scott, Principal

Lennoxville, PQ
J1M 1Z7

Bissoondath, Neil
author

c/o The Lucinda Vardey Agency
297 Seaton St.
Toronto, ON M5A 2T6

BiWay Stores Ltd.
Eric Paul, Chairman
discount retail chain

115 Commander Blvd.
Scarborough, ON M1S 3M7

Black, Arthur
host, CBC Radio's "Basic Black"

c/o CBC–Basic Black
P.O. Box 500, Stn. A
Toronto, ON M5W 1E6

Black, Conrad
Chairman, Hollinger Inc.
media mogul

10 Toronto St.
Toronto, ON M5C 2B7

Black Cultural Centre for Nova Scotia
Alma Johnston, President

P.O. Box 2128 East Postal
East Postal Station
Dartmouth, NS B2W 3Y2

Blais, Marie-Claire
author

448 ch. Sims
Kingsbury, PQ J0B 1X0

Blaise, Clark
author

c/o HarperCollins
10 East 53rd St.
New York, NY 10022
U.S.A.

Blake, Mervyn
actor

287 Huron Rd.
Sebringville, ON N0K 1X0

Blakeney, Alan
former Premier of Saskatchewan

1752 Prince of Wales Ave.
Saskatoon, SK S7K 3E5

Bliss, Michael
author/historian

314 Bessborough Dr.
Toronto, ON M4G 3L1

Bloc Québécois
Lucien Bouchard,
Leader and President

425 de Maisonneuve ouest
14ème étage
Montreal, PQ H3A 3G5

Blohm, Hans-Ludwig
photographer

64 Avonlea Rd.
Nepean, ON K2G 0J5

Blondin-Andrew, Ethel
federal Liberal Cabinet Minister from the NWT/*first native Canadian federal Cabinet Minister*

Room 252-WB
House of Commons
Ottawa, ON K1A 0A6

Blue Rodeo
rock group

25 Draper St.
Toronto, ON M5V 2M3

The Bluenose II
Capt. Douglas Himmelman,
skipper of the world-renowned tall ship

c/o Nova Scotia Department
Tourism, Culture and
Recreation
P.O. Box 456
Halifax, NS B3J 2R5

Bluteau, Lothaire
actor

c/o E. Klush Productions
5677 Hutchison Ave.
Montreal, PQ H2V 4B5

BMW Canada Inc.
Ed Robinson, President

920 Champlain Court
Whitby, ON L1N 6K9

B'nai Brith Canada
Marilyn Wainberg, President

15 Hove St.
Downsview, ON M3H 4Y8

Boggs, Jean Sutherland
art expert

P.O. Box 395, Stn. A
Ottawa, ON K1N 8V4

Bohlen, Jim and Phylis
Greenpeace founders

c/o Greenpeace Canada
185 Spadina Ave., 6th fl.
Toronto, ON M5T 2C6

Bolduc, Roch
Conservative Senator
from Quebec

Room 577-F
The Senate
Ottawa, ON K1A 0A4

Bombardier
Laurent Beaudoin,
Chairman and CEO
the Ski-Doo inventors

800 boul. René-Lévesque ouest,
Ste. 1700
Montreal, PQ H3B 1Y8

Bombardier, Denise
TV journalist/author

c/o SRC—Raison Passion
C.P. 6000
Montreal, PQ H3C 3A8

Bondar, Roberta
Professor of Medicine
second Canadian astronaut

Faculty of Health Sciences
McMaster University
Hamilton, ON L8S 4L8

Bonisteel, Roy
*broadcaster/*host Emeritus,
"Man Alive"

R.R. #5
Trenton, ON K8V 5P8

Bonnell, M. Lorne
Liberal Senator from P.E.I.

Room 265-E
The Senate
Ottawa, ON K1A 0A4

BootSauce
rock group

c/o The Agency
41 Britain St., Ste. 200
Toronto, ON M5A 1R7

Born With A Tooth, Milton
leader, Lonefighter Society
Oldman River development opponent

P.O. Box 70
Brocket, AB T0K 0H0

Borovoy, Alan *civil libertarian/author*	#403, 229 Yonge St. Toronto, ON M5B 1N9
Bosa, Peter Liberal Senator from Ontario	Room 246-N The Senate Ottawa, ON K1A 0A4
Bosley, John William former Speaker of the House of Commons and Conservative MP from Ontario	429 Lansdowne Rd. N., Rockcliffe, ON K1M 0X8
Bothwell, Robert S. *historian*	Trinity College 6 Hoskin Ave. Toronto, ON M5S 1H8
Botsford, Sara *actress*	c/o Lambur Talent Inc. 97 Browning Ave. Toronto, ON M4K 1W2
Bouchard, Benoît Ambassador to France/former federal Conservative Cabinet Minister from Quebec	Embassy of Canada 35, av. Montaigne 75008 Paris, France
Bouchard, Lucien Leader, Bloc Québécois and of the Official Opposition	Room 409-5 House of Commons Ottawa, ON K1A 0A6
Boucher, Gaétan *Olympic speed skater*	c/o Jandec 3080 le Carrefour, #800 Laval, PQ H7T 2R5
Bouey, Gerald former Governor, Bank of Canada	79 Kamploops Ave. Ottawa, ON K1V 7C8
Bourassa, Robert former Premier of Quebec	885 Grand-Allée est Bldg. J, 3rd fl. Quebec, PQ G1A 1A2
Bourgault, Jean-Julien *artist/sculptor*	St.-Jean-Port-Joli PQ G0R 3G0
Bourgault, Pierre *Quebec sovereigntist/poet*	Université de Québec à Montréal Facultie des Communications C.P. 8888, Succ. A Montreal, PQ H3C 3P8

Bower, Johnny
former Toronto Maple Leaf goalie

c/o Hockey Hall of Fame
BCE Place
30 Yonge St.
Toronto, ON M5E 1X8

Bowering, George
poet/author

2499 W. 37 Ave.
Vancouver, BC V6M 1P4

Bowker, Marjorie
retired judge/free trade opponent

10925, 85 Ave.
Edmonton, AB T6G 0W3

Bowling Federation of Canada
Al Hong, Executive Director

#3, 1475 Star Top Rd.
Gloucester, ON K1B 3W5

Bowman, Scotty
NHL coach with most wins in history

c/o Detroit Red Wings
Joe Louis Arena
Detroit, MI 48226
U.S.A.

The Box
rock group

c/o 41 Britain St., Ste. 305
Toronto, ON M5A 1R7

Boyd, George
newscaster, CBC "Newsworld"

c/o CBC–Newsworld
P.O. Box 500, Stn. A
Toronto, ON M5W 1E6

Boyd, Liona
classical guitarist/composer

c/o SOCAN
41 Valleybrook Dr.
Toronto, ON M3B 2S6

Boyle, Harry J.
writer/broadcaster

12 Georgian Court
Toronto, ON M4P 2J8

Brandon University
Dennis Anderson, President

Brandon, MB R7A 6A9

Brascan Ltd.
Peter F. Bronfman, Chairman

P.O. Box 129
Commerce Court W.
Toronto, ON M5L 1K5

Brasseur, Isabelle
figure skating champion

c/o IMG, 22 East 71st St.
New York, NY 10021, U.S.A.

Brault, Michel
film director

1168 Richelieu Beloeil
Quebec City, PQ J3G 4R3

Breslin, Mark
Founder and President, Yuk Yuk's comedy clubs

1280 Bay St.
Toronto, ON M5R 2C3

British American Bank Note Inc.
Dave Duncan, President
paper currency printers
P.O. Box 399, Stn. A
Ottawa, ON K1N 8V4

British Columbia Hydro and Power Authority (BC Hydro)
Marc Eliesen, CEO
970 Burrard St.
Vancouver, BC V6Z 1Y3

British Columbia Rail
P.J. McElligott,
CEO and President
Canada's third-largest railway
P.O. Box 8770
Vancouver, BC V6B 4X6

British Columbia Telephone Co. (BC Tel)
Gordon MacFarlane, Chairman
3777 Kingsway
Burnaby, BC V5H 3Z7

Broadbent, Edward
President, International Centre for Human Rights and Democratic Development/former federal NDP Leader
63 rue de Brésoles
Montreal, PQ H2Y 1V7

Broadfoot, Dave
comedian/"Royal Canadian Air Farce"
7 Hillholm Rd.
Toronto, ON M5P 1M1

Brochu, André
author
53 av. Wicksteed
Ville Mont-Royal, PQ
H3P 1P9

Brock University
Terrence White, President
500 Glenridge Ave.
St. Catharines, ON L2S 3A1

Bromley, David Allan
physicist/Assistant to the President for Science and Technology
c/o Yale University
A.W. Wright Nuclear Labs
272 Whitney St.
New Haven, CT 06511, U.S.A.

Bronfman, Charles Rosner
Chairman,
Executive Committee,
The Seagram Co. Ltd.
1430 Peel St.
Montreal, PQ H3A 1S9

Bronfman, Edgar Miles
industrialist/Chairman and CEO, The Seagram Co. Ltd./President, World Jewish Congress

375 Park Ave.
New York, NY 10152-0002
U.S.A.

Bronfman, Edward
Director, Edper Enterprises Ltd.

P.O. Box 778
BCE Place, 181 Bay St.
Toronto, ON M5J 2T3

Bronfman, Peter
Chairman, Edper Enterprises Ltd.

P.O. Box 778
BCE Place, 181 Bay St.
Toronto, ON M5J 2T3

Bronstein, Naomi
founder, Canada House Orphanage, Cambodia

Rue 278, No. 46
5th Group
Phnom Penh, Cambodia

Brooks, Bob
photographer

22 Covington Way
Halifax, NS B3M 3K2

Brossard, Nicole
author

34 av. Robert
Outremont, PQ H3S 2P2

Brott, Alexander
conductor/composer

5459 Earnscliffe Ave.
Montreal, PQ H3X 2P8

Brown, Ian
author/broadcaster

c/o 87 Gorevale Ave.
Toronto, ON M6J 2R5

Brown, Patrick J.
CBC News *correspondent*

43/51 Great Titichfield St.
London W1
England

Brown, Rosemary
President, Ontario Human Rights Commission/*first black woman elected to political office in Canada*

400 University Ave.
Toronto, ON M7A 2R9

Browning, Kurt
world champion Olympic skater

c/o Canadian Figure Skating Association
1600 James Naismith Dr.
Ste. 403
Gloucester, ON K1B 5N4

Bruce, Harry
author/journalist

General Delivery
St. Andrews, NB E0G 2X0

Buchanan, John Conservative Senator/ former Premier of Nova Scotia	Room 271-EB The Senate Ottawa, ON K1A 0A4
Budd, Barbara co-host, CBC's "As It Happens"	c/o CBC–As It Happens P.O. Box 500, Stn. A Toronto, ON M5W 1E6
Buddhist Churches of Canada Roi Akune, President	260 12830 Clarke Place Richmond, BC V6V 2H5
Bujold, Geneviève *actress*	c/o William Morris Agency 151 El Camino Beverly Hills, CA 90212 U.S.A.
Burdette, Paul *world-renowned wood carver*	c/o Burdette Gallery R.R. #2 Orton, ON L0N 1N0
Burka, Petra *world figure skating champion*	13 Bushey Ave. Toronto, ON M6N 2R4
Burns, John *The New York Times* correspondent	229 West 43rd St. New York, NY 10036 U.S.A.
Business Council on National Issues Thomas d'Aquino, President and CEO	806 Royal Bank Centre 90 Sparks St. Ottawa, ON K1P 5B4
Butala, Sharon *author*	P.O. Box 428 Eastend, SK S0N 0T0
Butler, Edith *Acadian singer/songwriter*	86, ch. de la Côte Ste-Catherine Montreal, PQ H2V 2A3
Butler, Rob *first Canadian to appear for a Canadian team in the World Series* (1993)	c/o Toronto Blue Jays 300 The Esplanade W., Ste. 3200 Toronto, ON M5V 3B3
Byfield, Ted owner and Publisher, *The Alberta Report*	17327–106A Ave. NW Edmonton, AB T5S 9Z9

C

"Letters are expectation packaged in an envelope."

Shana Alexander

Cadieux, Léo
former federal Liberal Cabinet
Minister from Quebec
diplomat

20 The Driveway
Ottawa, ON K2P 1C8

Caisse de dépôt et placement du Québec
Jean-Claude Delorme, Chairman

1981 av. McGill College
Montreal, PQ H3A 3C7

Calder, Frank Arthur
first Native Indian elected to a Canadian Legislature (B.C., 1949) and to serve as a Cabinet Minister

1060 St. David St.
Victoria, BC V8S 4Y8

Calemeadow Foundation
Mary Cole, Executive Director
promotes self-employment among those in need

4 King Street W.
Toronto, ON M5H 1B6

Calgary Exhibition and Stampede
Danny Copithorne, President
"The Greatest Outdoor Show on Earth"

P.O. Box 1860, Stn. M
Calgary, AB T2P 2L8

Calgary Flames Hockey Club
Doug Risebrough,
General Manager

The Saddledome
P.O. Box 1540, Stn. M
Calgary, AB T2P 3B9

Calgary Herald
Kevin Peterson, Publisher

P.O. Box 2400, Stn. M
Calgary, AB T2P 0W8

Calgary Stampeders Football Club
Wally Buono, General Manager
1817 Crowchild Trail N.W.
Calgary, AB T2M 4R6

The Calgary Sun
Ken King, Publisher
2615 12th St. N.E.
Calgary, AB T2E 7W9

Callaghan, Barry
author
20 Dale Ave.
Toronto, ON M4W 1K4

Callbeck, Catherine
Premier of P.E.I./
former Liberal MP
The Premier's Office
P.O. Box 2000
Charlottetown, PE C1A 7N8

Callwood, June
author/journalist/humanitarian
21 Hillcroft Dr.
Islington, ON M9B 4X4

Call-Net Telecommunications Ltd.
Juri Koor, CEO
Canada's largest reseller of telephone services
105 Gordon Baker Rd.
Toronto, ON M2H 3P8

Calm Air International Ltd.
northern Canadian airline
90 Thompson Dr.
Thompson, MB R8N 1Y8

Cameron, A.M. Sandy
former Nova Scotia
Liberal Leader
P.O. Box 70
Sherbrooke, NS B0J 3C0

Cameron, Bill
broadcast journalist
c/o CBC News
P.O. Box 500, Stn. A
Toronto, ON M5W 1E6

Cameron, Donald
Canadian Consul General in
New England/former Premier
of Nova Scotia
3 Copley Place, Ste. 400
Boston, MA 02116
U.S.A.

Cameron, Elspeth MacGregor
author/journalist
University College
15 Kings College Circle
University of Toronto
Toronto, ON M5S 1A1

Cameron, Dr. Jim
beaver expert
Dept. of Geography
York University
4700 Keele St.
North York, ON M3J 1P3

Cameron, John Allan
singer/songwriter
c/o Brooks Diamond Productions
1819 Granville St., 4th fl.
Halifax, NS B3J 3R1

Cameron, Silver Donald
author/broadcaster
D'Escousse, NS B0E 1K0

Camp, Dalton
Conservative Party adviser/ political commentator
Cambridge Northwood
Queens Co., NB E0E 1B0

Campaign Life Coalition
Jim Hughes, National President
1355 Wellington St.
Ottawa, ON K1Y 3C2

Campbell, Gordon
Leader, B.C Liberal Party/
former Mayor of Vancouver
Legislative Assembly of
British Columbia
Parliament Buildings
Victoria, BC V8V 1X4

Campbell, Kim
first woman Prime Minister of Canada (1993)
c/o Conservative Party of Canada
200, 161 Laurier Ave. W.
Ottawa, ON K1P 5J2

Campbell Soup Co.
Daniel O'Neill
President and CEO
60 Birmingham St.
Toronto, ON M8V 2B8

Campeau, Robert
former real estate developer
29 Unterburgauy
St. Gilgen, Austria

Canada AM
morning current affairs show
c/o CTV
P.O. Box 3000
Agincourt, ON M1S 3C6

Canada Council
Paul Leduc, Director
99 Metcalfe St.
P.O. Box 1047
Ottawa, ON K1P 5V8

Canada Deposit Insurance Corporation (CDIC)
Grant L. Reuber, Chairman
P.O. Box 2340, Stn. D
Ottawa, ON K1P 5W5

Canada Post Corporation
Donald H. Lander,
Chairman and CEO
720 Heron Rd.
Ottawa, ON K1A 0B1

Canada Publishing Corporation
Ron Besse,
Chairman, President and CEO
164 Commander Blvd.
Agincourt, ON M1S 3C7

Canada Trust Edmund Clark, President and CEO *Canada's largest trust company*	P.O. Box 5703, Stn. A London, ON N6A 4S4
Canadian Abortion Rights Action League Jane Holmes, Executive Co-ordinator	#306, 344 Bloor St. W. Toronto, ON M5S 3A7
Canadian Academy of Recording Arts and Sciences Daisy Falle, Executive Director	124 Merton St., 3rd fl. Toronto, ON M4S 2Z2
Canadian Advanced Technology Association John Reid, President	388 Albert St. 3rd fl. Ottawa, ON K1R 5B2
Canadian Advisory Council on the Status of Women Glenda Simms, President	P.O. Box 1541, Stn. B Ottawa, ON K1P 5R5
Canadian AIDS Society Richard Burzynski, Executive Director	100 Sparks St., Ste. 701 Ottawa, ON K1P 5B7
Canadian Airlines International Kevin Jenkins, President	2800–700 2 St. S.W. Calgary, AB T2P 2W2
Canadian Alliance in Solidarity with the Native Peoples Jimmy Dick, National Co-ordinator	P.O. Box 574, Stn. P Toronto, ON M5S 2T1
Canadian Association of the Deaf Shelly Carver, President	205–2435 Holly Lane Ottawa, ON K1V 7P2
Canadian Association of Elizabeth Fry Societies Claude Bernier, President	251 Bank St., Ste. 600 Ottawa, ON K2P 1X3
Canadian Authors Association Jeffrey Holmes, National Director	275 Slater St., #500 Ottawa, ON K1P 5H9

Canadian Automobile Association (CAA) Michael S. McNeil, President	1775 Courtwood Cres. Ottawa, ON K2C 3J2
Canadian Auto Workers Union (CAW) Buzz Hargrove, President	205 Placer Ct. Willowdale, ON M2H 3H9
Canadian Bankers Association (CBA) Helen K. Sinclair, President	P.O. Box 348 2 First Canadian Place Toronto, ON M5X 1E1
Canadian Bar Association Cecilia Johnstone, President	50 O'Connor St., Ste. 902 Ottawa, ON K1P 6L2
Canadian Baton Twirling Federation Deardra Leslie, Technical Director	156 Duke St. W. Kitchener, ON N2H 3X1
Canadian Bible Society Rev. Floyd Babcock, Canadian General Secretary	10 Carnforth Rd. Toronto, ON M4A 2S4
Canadian Brass *brass ensemble*	40 Alexandra St., P2 Toronto, ON M4Y 1B5
Canadian Broadcasting Corporation (CBC) Tony Manera President and CEO	P.O. Box 8478 Ottawa, ON K1G 3J5
Canadian Bureau for International Education James W. Fox, President	Ste. 1400, 85 Albert St. Ottawa, ON K1P 6A4
***Canadian Business* magazine** Randall Litchfield, Editor	70 The Esplanade, Ste. 214 Toronto, ON M5E 1R2
Canadian Cancer Society Douglas H. Barr, CEO	10 Alcorn Ave., Ste. 200 Toronto, ON M4V 3B1
Canadian Centre for Drug-Free Sport Victor Lachance, CEO	1600 James Naismith Dr. Ste. 702 Gloucester, ON K1B 5N4
Canadian Centre for Global Security Stanley Urman, Executive Director	151 Slater St., Ste. 710 Ottawa, ON K1P 5H3

Canadian Centre for Policy Alternatives
Duncan Cameron, President
251 Laurier Ave. W., #804
Ottawa, ON K1P 5J6

Canadian Centre for Victims of Torture
Joan Simalchik, Executive Director
40 Westmoreland Ave.
Toronto, ON M6H 2Z7

Canadian Centre on Substance Abuse
H. David Archibald, Chairman of the Board
112 Kent St., Ste. 480
Ottawa, ON K1P 5P2

Canadian Chamber of Commerce
Tim Reid, President
55 Metcalfe St., Ste. 1160
Ottawa, ON K1P 6N4

Canadian Children's Foundation
Heather Sproule, Executive Director
60 Bloor St. W., #1011
Toronto ON M4W 1A1

Canadian Civil Liberties Association
Sybil Shack, President
#403, 229 Yonge St.
Toronto, ON M5B 1N9

Canadian Conference of the Arts
Keith Kelly, National Director
189 Laurier Ave. E.
Ottawa, ON K1N 6P1

***Canadian Consumer* magazine**
John Marteinson, Editor
Box 9300, Stn. T
Ottawa, ON K1G 3T9

Canadian Council for International Cooperation
Robert Logan, Executive Director
1 Nicholas St., Ste. 300
Ottawa, ON K1N 7B7

Canadian Council for Racial Harmony
Jeffrey S. Ram, President
P.O. Box 190, Stn. J
Toronto, ON M4J 4Y1

Canadian Council of Better Business Bureaus
Wayne Lovely, President
2180 Steeles Ave. W., #219
Concord, ON L4K 2Z5

Canadian Council of Christians and Jews Elyse Graff, National Executive Director	44 Victoria St., Ste. 1800 Toronto, ON M5C 1Y2
Canadian Council of Churches Stuart E. Brown, General Secretary	40 St. Clair Ave. E. Ste. 210 Toronto, ON M4T 1M9
Canadian Country Music Hall of Fame	P.O. Box 1660, Stn. C Kitchener, ON N2G 4R2
Canadian Curling Association Dave Parkes, General Manager	1600 James Naismith Dr. #803 Gloucester, ON K1B 5N4
Canadian Direct Marketing Association *removes names from junk-mail lists*	1 Concorde Gate Don Mills, ON M3C 3N6
Canadian Donkey and Mule Association George H. France, President	c/o Greynose Farm R.R. #2, Acton, ON L7J 2L8
Canadian Ethnocultural Council Anna Chiappa, Executive Director	#1100 251 Laurier Ave. W. Ottawa, ON K1P 5J6
Canadian Exporters' Assoc. Mark Drake, President	99 Bank St., Ste. 250 Ottawa, ON K1P 6B9
Canadian Federation of Independent Business John Bulloch, President	4141 Yonge St., Ste. 401 Willowdale, ON M2P 2A6
Canadian Football Hall of Fame and Museum Ed Chalupka, Managing Director	58 Jackson Street W. Hamilton, ON L8P 1L4
Canadian Football League (CFL) Larry Smith, Commissioner	110 Eglinton Ave. W. Toronto, ON M4R 1A3
***Canadian Forum* magazine** Duncan Cameron, Editor	5502 Atlantic St. Halifax, NS B3H 1G4
Canadian Foundation for AIDS Research Bluma Appel, Chairperson	120 Bloor St., 1st fl. Toronto, ON M4W 1B8

Canadian Foundation on Compulsive Gambling
Tibor I. Barsony,
Executive Director
#605, 505 Consumers Rd.
Willowdale, ON M2J 4V8

Canadian 4-H Council
Betsy Clarke, Executive Director
#208, 1690 Woodward Dr.
Ottawa, ON K2C 3R8

***Canadian Geographic* magazine**
Ian Darragh, Editor
39 McArthur St.
Vanier, ON K1L 8L7

Canadian Give the Gift of Literacy Foundation
Kathy Lowinger, Chairperson
35 Spadina Rd.
Toronto, ON M5R 2S9

Canadian Guide Dogs for the Blind
Bill Thorton, President
4120 Rideau Valley Dr. N.
Manotick, ON K4M 1A3

Canadian Hearing Society
Gordon Ryall, Executive Director
271 Spadina Rd.
Toronto, ON M5R 2V3

Canadian Home Shopping Network (CHSN)
Simon Paul Dean,
President and CEO
1400 Castlefield Ave.
Toronto, ON M6B 4H8

Canadian Human Rights Commission
Max Yalden, Chief Commissioner
320 Queen St.
Ottawa, ON K1A 1E1

Canadian Hunger Foundation
Bruce Moore, Executive Director
323 Chapel St.
Ottawa, ON K1N 7Z2

Canadian Imperial Bank of Commerce (CIBC)
Bob Peterson,
Chairman and CEO
Canada's second-largest bank
Commerce Court
Toronto, ON M5L 1A2

Canadian Institute of International Affairs (CIIA)
Alex Morrison,
Executive Director
15 King's College Circle
Toronto, ON M5S 2V9

Canadian Institute of Strategic Studies
Don Macnamara, President
76 St. Clair Ave. W.
Ste. 502
Toronto, ON M4V 1N2

Canadian International Development Agency (CIDA)
Jocelyne Bourgon, President
200 Promenade du Portage
Hull, PQ K1A 0G4

Canadian Jewish Congress
Irving Abella, President
1590 av. Docteur Penfield
Montreal, PQ H3G 1C5

Canadian Labour Congress (CLC)
Bob White, President
2841 Riverside Dr.
Ottawa, ON K1V 8X7

Canadian League of Urban Butches (CLUB)
Cathy Askim, President
organization for the woman who wants to "Be in Total Control of Herself"
32 Marley Place
London, ON N6C 3T2

***Canadian Living* magazine**
Bonnie Baker Cowan, Editor-in-Chief
50 Holly St.
Toronto, ON M4S 3B3

Canadian Manufacturers' Association
Stephen Van Houten, President
75 International Blvd.
4th fl.
Etobicoke, ON M9W 6L9

Canadian Medical Association
Dr. Richard Kennedy, President
1867 Alta Vista Dr.
P.O. Box 8650
Ottawa, ON K1G 3Y6

Canadian Museum of Caricature
Jim Burant, Curator
136 St. Patrick St.
Ottawa, ON K1N 5J8

Canadian Museum of Civilization
George F. MacDonald, Director
P.O. Box 3100, Stn. B
Hull, PQ J8X 4H2

Canadian Museum of Nature
Dr. Alan R. Emery, Director
P.O. Box 3443, Stn. D
Ottawa, ON K1P 6P4

Canadian National Exhibition (CNE)
Richard G. Stackhouse, President
Exhibition Place
Toronto, ON M6K 3C3

Canadian National Institute for the Blind (CNIB)
Dr. Euclid J. Herie, President and CEO
1931 Bayview Ave.
Toronto, ON M4G 4C8

Canadian National Railway Co. (CNR) Paul M. Tellier, CEO	935 de la Gauchetière ouest Montreal, PQ H3B 2M9
Canadian Nature Federation Julie Gelfand, Executive Director	453 Sussex Dr. Ottawa, ON K1N 6Z4
Canadian Network for the Advancement of Research, Industry and Education (CANARIE) Rafiq Khan, Office Director *Canada's information highway developers*	c/o Stentor Telecom Policy Inc. 45 O'Conner St. Ottawa, ON K1P 1A4
Canadian Nuclear Association John M. Reid, President	77 Metcalfe St. Ottawa, ON K1P 4L6
Canadian Olympic Association Sherif Alaily, COO	2380 av. Pierre Dupuy Cité du Havre Montreal, PQ H3C 3R4
The Canadian Opera Company (COC)	227 Front St. E. Toronto, ON M5A 1EB
Canadian Organization for Development Through Education (CODE) Robert Dyck, National Director	321 Chapel St. Ottawa, ON K1N 7Z2
Canadian Pacific Ltd. William W. Stinson, Chairman and CEO	P.O. Box 6042, Stn. A Montreal, PQ H3C 3E4
Canadian Parents for French Jos Craven Scott, Executive Director	309 Cooper St., Ste. 210 Ottawa, ON K2P 0G5
Canadian Parks and Wilderness Society Harvey Locke, President	160 Bloor St. E., #1150 Toronto, ON M4W 1B9
Canadian Peace Alliance Gideon Forman, Co-ordinator	555 Bloor St. W., Ste. 5 Toronto, ON M5S 1Y6
Canadian Polo Association Michael Sifton, contact	c/o Armdale Co. Ltd. Toronto Buttonville Airport Markham, ON L3P 3J9

Canadian Press Gordon Bullock, Chairman	36 King St. E. Toronto, ON M5C 2L9
Canadian Radio-television and Telecommunications Commission (CRTC) Keith Spicer, Chairman	1 Promenade du Portage Hull, PQ K1A 0N2
Canadian Real Estate Association David Higgins, President	320 Queen St., #2100 Ottawa, ON K1R 5A3
Canadian Recording Industry Association Brian Robertson, President	1255 Yonge St., #300 Toronto, ON M4T 1W6
Canadian Red Cross Society Douglas Lindores, Secretary General	1800 Alta Vista Dr. Ottawa, ON K1G 4J5
The Canadian Republic Movement *promotes the idea of a Republic of Canada*	P.O. Box 1510, Stn. A Kelowna, BC V1Y 7V8
Canadian Security Intelligence Service (CSIS) Ray Protti, Director	P.O. Box 9732 Postal Stn. T Ottawa, ON K1G 4G4
Canadian Ski Association Ron Payment, Executive Director	1600 James Naismith Dr. #401 Gloucester, ON K1B 5N4
Canadian Snowbird Association Jack Parry, President *tackles issues of interest to Canadians in Florida*	Atria North, #2 2235 Sheppard Ave. E. Box 54 North York, ON M2J 5B5
Canadian Society for the Prevention of Cruelty to Animals	5215 Jean Talon ouest Montreal, PQ H4P 1X4
Canadian Society for the Prevention of Cruelty to Children Dr. E.T. Barket, President	356 First St., Box 700 Midland, ON L4R 4P4

Canadian Society for the Study of Names
Wolfgang Ahrens
studies all aspects of names in Canada

Dept. of Languages
Literature and Linguistics
York University
4700 Keele St.
North York, ON M3J 1P3

Canadian Space Agency
Dr. Roland Doré, President

Place Air Canada
500 boul. René-Lévesque ouest
Montreal, PQ H2Z 1Z7

Canadian Special Olympics
Bill L'Heureux, Chairman

209 40 St. Clair Ave. W.
Toronto, ON M4V 1M6

Canadian Tax Foundation
Douglas J. Sherbaniuk, Director

1 Queen St. E., Ste. 1800
Toronto, ON M5C 2Y2

Canadian Tire Corp. Ltd.
Stephen Bachand,
President and CEO

P.O. Box 770, Stn. K
Toronto, ON M4P 2V8

Canadian Tulip Festival
Caroline Risi, Tourism Director
world's largest tulip festival

360 Albert St., Ste. 1720
Ottawa, ON K1R 7X7

Canadian University Services Overseas (CUSO)
Lyse Blanchard,
Executive Director

135 Rideau St.
Ottawa, ON K1N 9K7

Canadian Vietnam Veterans
Lee Hitchins, President

P.O. Box 11375, Stn. H
Nepean, ON K3H 7V1

Canadian Western Bank
Lawrence M. Pollock,
President and CEO
Canada's smallest domestically owned bank

10305 Jasper Ave.
Ste. 2300
Edmonton, AB T5J 3X6

Canadian Wildlife Federation
Jim Hook, President

2740 Queensview Dr.
Ottawa, ON K2B 1A2

Canadians Concerned About Violence in Entertainment (C-CAVE)
Rose Dyson, Chairperson

167 Glen Rd.
Toronto, ON M4W 2W8

Cancer Information Service
Patricia Payne, Manager

755 Concession St.
Ste. 201
Hamilton, ON L8V 1C4

Candy, John *actor/comedian*	8899 Beverley Blvd. Los Angeles, CA 90048, U.S.A.
Canstar Sports Inc. Donald MacMartan, CEO *world's largest hockey equipment manufacturer*	5705 Ferrier St., Ste. 200 Montreal, PQ H4P 1N3
Cape Breton's Magazine Ronald Caplan, Publisher	Wreck Cove NS B0C 1H0
Caplan, Gerry NDP adviser/*public affairs commentator*	146 Kamloops Ave. Ottawa, ON K1V 7C9
Carbonneau, Guy *hockey player*	c/o Montreal Canadiens 2313 Ste-Catherine ouest Montreal, PQ H3H 1N2
Cardinal, Douglas *architect*	55 Murray St., 6th fl. Ottawa, ON K1N 5M3
CARE Canada A. John Watson, Executive Director	P.O. Box 9000, Stn. T Ottawa, ON K1G 4X6
Careless, James M.S. *historian*	Dept. of History University of Toronto Toronto, ON M5S 1A1
Caribana Samuel Lewis, Chairman *Caribbean cultural festival*	171 Carlton St., Ste. 200 Toronto, ON M5A 2K3
Carle, Gilles *film producer*	c/o ARRFQ 122, 1600 rue de Lorimier Montreal, PQ H2K 3W5
Carleton University Robin Farquhar, President	Colonel By Dr. Ottawa, ON K1S 5B6
Carney, Pat Conservative Senator from B.C./ former federal Cabinet Minister	Room 483-S The Senate Ottawa, ON K1A 0A4
Carr, Shirley *former labour leader*	c/o 2841 Riverside Dr. Ottawa, ON K1V 8X7
Carrier, Roch *author*	3785 Harvard St. Montreal, PQ H4A 2W6

Carstairs, Sharon
former Manitoba Liberal Leader

Room 172
Legislative Assembly
Winnipeg, MB R3C 0V8

Carter, His Eminence G. Emmett
Cardinal (R.C.)/Archbishop
Emeritus of Toronto

c/o 355 Church St.
Toronto, ON M5B 1Z8

Carter, Graydon
Editor, *Vanity Fair*

350 Madison Ave.
New York, NY 10017, U.S.A.

Carter, Wilf
country singer

c/o Clair Dezan
Wilf Carter Fan Club
P.O. Box 53
Ayer's Cliff, PQ J0B 1C0

Cashin, Richard
former Newfoundland
labour leader

2 Steers Cove
St. John's, NF A1C 6J5

Cassleman-Wadds, Jean
former Conservative MP and
High Commissioner to
Great Britain

P.O. Box 579
Prescott, ON K0E 1T0

Castonguay, Claude
former Conservative Senator
from Quebec

Laurentian Bank of Canada
1981 McGill College Ave.
Montreal, PQ H3A 3K3

Catley-Carlson, Margaret
President, Population Council/
former President of CIDA

1 Dag Hammarskjold Plaza
New York, NY 10017
U.S.A.

C.D. Howe Institute
Tom Kierans, President and CEO
economics and public policy
think tank

125 Adelaide St. E.
Toronto, ON M5C 1L7

Centre de Recherches
sur l'Opinion Publique (CROP)
Alain Gigure, President
polling organization

500–651 Notre Dame ouest
Montreal, PQ H3C 1H8

Century 21 Real Estate
Canada Ltd.
Uwe Gary Charlwood,
Chairman and CEO

135–10551 Shellbridge Way
Richmond, BC V6X 2W9

Chalk Circle *rock group*	P.O. Box 1059, Stn. F Toronto, ON M4Y 2T7
Champ, Henry co-host, "CBC Morning News"	c/o CBC–Newsworld P.O. Box 500, Stn. A Toronto, ON M5W 1E6
Chang, Simon *fashion designer*	555 Richmond St. W. Toronto, ON M5V 3B1
Chang, Thomas Ming Swi *medical scientist*	Artificial Cells and Organs Research Centre McGill University 3655 Drummond St. Montreal, PQ H3G 1Y6
Chapleau, Serge *editorial cartoonist*	c/o *Le Devoir* 211 Ste-Sacrement Montreal, PQ H2Y 1X1
Chaput-Rolland, Solange Conservative Senator from Quebec *author/journalist*	50 av. Bernard St-Sauveur, PQ J0R 1R0
Charbonneau, Guy Conservative Senator from Quebec	Room 280-F The Senate Ottawa, ON K1A 0A4
Charest, Jean Leader, Conservative Party of Canada, MP/former Cabinet Minister from Quebec	Room 436-N House of Commons Ottawa, ON K1A 0A6
Charles, HRH Prince Prince of Wales/ Heir to the Throne	Highgrove Daughton Tethleway, Gloucestershire GL8 8TG, England
***Chatelaine* magazine** Mildred Istona, Editor	777 Bay St. Toronto, ON M5W 1A7
Chen, Wei news anchor, CTV's "Canada AM"	c/o CTV–Canada AM P.O. Box 3000 Agincourt, ON M1S 3C6
Cherry, Don *sports commentator*	88 Wilson St. W., Ste. 2A Ancaster, ON L9G 1N2
Chess Federation of Canada Gordon Taylor, Executive Director	2212 Gladwin Cres., E-1 Ottawa, ON K1B 5N1

Chesterfield, Norm
world's leading birdwatcher
R.R. #3
Wheatley, ON N0P 2P0

Chevalier, Leo
fashion designer
P.O. Box 1240, Stn. H
Montreal, PQ H3G 1N7

Chiarelli, Rita
blues singer
300 1670 Bayview Ave.
Toronto, ON M4G 3C2

Child Find Canada Inc.
Elizabeth Vi George, President
network that assists in locating abducted or missing children (1-800-387-7962 for clients and sightings only)
1002 Arlington St., Ste. 41
Saskatoon, SK S7H 2X7

Children's Wish Foundation of Canada
Laura Cole, Executive Director
fulfils wishes of children with life-threatening illnesses
1735 Bayly St., Ste. 8C
Pickering, ON L1W 3G7

Chilton, David
author of *The Wealthy Barber*
660 Deer Run Dr.
Waterloo, ON N2K 3H3

Chiriaeff, Ludmilla
Founder, Les Grands Ballets Canadiens
4816 rue Rivard
Montreal, PQ H2J 2N6

Chong, Tom
"Cheech and Chong"
actor/comedian
c/o Monterey Peninsula Artists
P.O. Box 7308
Carmel, CA 93921-7308, U.S.A.

Chouinard, Josée
figure skating champion
c/o IMG
1 St. Clair Ave. E., #700
Toronto, ON M4T 2V7

Chouinard, Marie
choreographer/dancer
3981 boul. St-Laurent
Ste. 615
Montreal, PQ H2W 1Y5

Chrétien, Jean
Prime Minister/Leader, Liberal Party of Canada
Langevin Block
80 Wellington St.
Ottawa, ON K1A 0A2

Chrétien, Raymond
Ambassador to the United States
Canadian Embassy
501 Pennsylvania Ave. N.W.
Washington, DC 20001 U.S.A.

Christian Heritage Party of Canada
Heather Stilwell, Leader

#203, 20651 51 Ave.
Langley, BC V3A 3Y9

Christie, Dinah
singer/film and stage performer

R.R. #1
Holstein, ON N0G 2A0

Chronicle Herald
Jane Purves, Managing Editor

P.O. Box 610
Halifax, NS B3J 2T2

Chrysler Canada Ltd.
G. Yves Landry,
President and CEO

2450 Chrysler Centre
Windsor, ON N9A 4H6

Church of Jesus Christ of Latter-Day Saints (Mormons)
Richard Robertson,
Director of Public Affairs

234–7181 Woodbine Ave.
Markham ON L3R 1A3

Chuvalo, George
former boxer

46 Golfwood Heights
Weston, ON M9P 3M2

Cinader, Bernard
geneticist/biochemist

Medical Science Bldg.
University of Toronto
Toronto, ON M5S 1A8

Cineplex-Odeon
Alan Karp, CEO

1303 Yonge St.
Toronto, ON M4T 2Y9

Cirque de Soleil
Gilles Ste-Croix,
Creative Director
avant-garde circus

Les Productions du
Cirque de Soleil
1217 Notre-Dame est
Montreal, PQ H2L 2R3

Cité Libre
Jean-Pierre Goyer, Editor

1250 boul. René-Lévesque ouest
Montreal, PQ H3B 4Y1

Citizens Concerned About Free Trade
David Orchard,
National Chairman

P.O. Box 8052
Saskatoon, SK S7K 4R7

Clark, Joe
former Conservative Prime Minister/Professor of Canadian-American Relations

c/o Dept. of Political Science
University of California
Berkeley, CA 94720
U.S.A.

Clark, Wendel
hockey player
c/o Toronto Maple Leafs
60 Carlton St.
Toronto, ON M5B 1L1

Clarke, Austin
author
62 McGill St.
Toronto, ON M5B 1H2

Clarkson, Adrienne
host, CBC's "Adrienne Clarkson Presents"
c/o CBC
P.O. Box 500, Stn. A
Toronto, ON M5W 1E6

Clarkson, Stephen
author
44 Rosedale Rd.
Toronto, ON M4W 2P6

CN Tower
world's tallest freestanding structure
301 Front St. W.
Toronto, ON M5V 2J5

Coady International Institute
Eric Amit, Director
promotes co-operatives and credit unions and the organization of people to take control of the local economy
c/o St. Francis Xavier University
Antigonish, NS B2G 1C0

Coca-Cola Canada Ltd.
Anthony G. Eames,
President and CEO
1 Concorde Gate, Ste. 500
Don Mills, ON M3C 3N6

Cochrane, Ethel
Conservative Senator from Newfoundland
Room 357-S
The Senate
Ottawa, ON K1A 0A4

Cochrane, Tom
rock musician
P.O. Box 212
Islington, ON M9A 4X2

Cockburn, Bruce
folk/rock singer/musician
Finkelstein Mgmt. Co. Ltd.
151 John St., Ste. 301
Toronto, ON M5V 2T2

Cogger, Michel
Conservative Senator from Quebec
Room 489-S
The Senate
Ottawa, ON K1A 0A4

Cognos Inc.
Michael Potter,
Chairman and CEO
Canada's largest independent software maker
3755 Riverside Dr.
Ottawa, ON K1G 3Z4

Cohen, Erminie
Conservative Senator from New Brunswick

Room 806-VB
The Senate
Ottawa, ON K1A 0A4

Cohen, Leonard
poet/author/songwriter

c/o Stranger Music Inc.
419 North Larchmont Blvd.
Ste. 91
Los Angeles, CA 90004
U.S.A.

Cohen, Marshall "Mickey"
President and CEO, The Molson Companies Ltd.

Scotia Plaza
40 King St. W., Ste. 3600
Toronto, ON M5H 3Z5

Cohen, Matt
author

P.O. Box 401
Verona, ON K0H 2W0

Cohen, Maxwell
international law expert

200 Rideau Terrace,
Apt. 1404
Ottawa, ON K1M 0Z3

Cohon, George A.
Senior Chairman, McDonald's Restaurants of Canada

McDonald's Place
Toronto, ON M3C 3L4

Cole, Holly
jazz singer

c/o Alert Management
41 Britain St., Ste. 305
Toronto, ON M5A 1R7

Coleman, John
Canadian Executive Director, European Bank for Reconstruction and Development (EBRD)

c/o EBRD
122 Leadenhall St.
London EC3V 4EB, England

Collenette, David
federal Liberal Cabinet Minister from Ontario

Room 121-EB
House of Commons
Ottawa, ON K1A 0A6

Colombo, John Robert
author/Canadiana expert/anthologist

42 Dell Park Ave.
Toronto, ON M6B 2T6

Colville, Alex
artist

P.O. Box 550
408 Main St.
Wolfville, NS B0P 1XO

Comeau, Gerald Conservative Senator from Nova Scotia	Room 546-N The Senate Ottawa, ON K1A 0A4
Commonwealth Games Association of Canada Dr. Ivor Dent, President	1600 James Naismith Dr. Ste. 308 Gloucester, ON K1B 5N4
Communications Security Establishment (CSE) A.S. Woolner, Chief *surveillance agency*	Confederation Heights 719 Heron Rd. Ottawa, ON K1A 0K2
Communist Party of Canada Miguel Figueroa, Leader	24 Cecil St. Toronto, ON M5T 1N2
Concordia University Patrick Kenniff, Rector	1463 rue Bishop, Pièce 201 Montreal, PQ H3G 2E4
Confederacy of Mainland Micmacs Dan Paul, Leader	P.O. Box 1590 Truro, NS B2N 5V3
Confederation of Regions Western Party (COR) Nora Galenzoski, Leader	4860–201 St. Langley, BC V3A 1P4
Conference Board of Canada Janes R. Nininger, President and CEO *economic think tank*	255 Smyth Rd. Ottawa, ON K1H 8M7
Connors, "Stompin' Tom" *folk singer*	c/o Brian Edwards P.O. Box 1282 Peterborough, ON K9J 7H5
Consumers' Association of Canada Marilyn Lister, President	307 Gilmour St. Ottawa, ON K2P 0P7
Consumers' Gas Co. Ltd. Robert W. Martin, President and CEO	P.O. Box 650 Scarborough, ON M1K 5E3
Cook, Ramsay *author/historian*	Dept. of History, York University 4700 Keele St. North York, ON M3J 1P3

Cooke, Jack Kent *billionaire/Washington Redskins owner*	Far Acres Middleburg, VA 22117 U.S.A.
Cools, Anne Liberal Senator from Ontario	Room 178-F The Senate Ottawa, ON K1A 0A4
Coon Come, Matthew Cree Grand Chief/Chairman, Grand Council of the Crees	3434–1, Place Ville Marie Montreal, PQ H3B 3N6
Cooper, Heather *illustrator/graphic designer*	P.O. Box 185, Stn. Q Toronto, ON M4T 2M1
Copps, Sheila Deputy Prime Minister and Liberal MP from Ontario	Room 511–S House of Commons Ottawa, ON K1A 0A6
Corbin, Eymard Liberal Senator from New Brunswick	Room 575-F The Senate Ottawa, ON K1A 0A4
Corcoran, Jim *rock singer*	c/o Spectra Scene 355 Ste.-Catherine ouest, Ste.700 Montreal, PQ H3B 1A5
Corel Corp. Michael C.J. Cowpland, President *CorelDraw software manufacturer*	1600 Carling Ave. Ottawa, ON K1Z 8R7
Cory, Peter Justice, Supreme Court of Canada	Supreme Court of Canada Wellington St. Ottawa, ON K1A 0J1
Cosmatos, George *film director/producer/ scriptwriter*	c/o ICM, 8899 Beverley Blvd. Los Angeles, CA 90048 U.S.A.
Costa, Carlos *first person with a disability to swim across Lake Ontario*	62 Lomar Dr. Downsview, ON M3W 1Z3
Costello, Brian *personal finance expert*	Hometax Information Systems 55 Adelaide St. E., Ste.402 Toronto, ON M5C 1K6

Cott Corporation
Gerry Pencer, Chairman
soft drink producer
946 Lakeshore Road E.
Mississauga, ON L5E 1E4

Council for Business and the Arts in Canada
Blair Mascall, President and CEO
401 Bay St., P.O. Box 7
Toronto, ON M5H 2Y4

Council of Canadians
Maude Barlow, Chairperson
nationalist organization
1006–251 Laurier St. W.
Ottawa, ON K1P 5J6

Country Music Foundation of Canada
William Maxim, Chairman
8607–128 Ave.
Edmonton, AB T5E 0G3

Coupland, Douglas
Generation X author
c/o McClelland & Stewart
481 University Ave., Ste. 900
Toronto, ON M5G 2E9

Cournoyea, Nellie
Northwest Territories
Government Leader
Legislative Assembly
P.O. Box 1320
Yellowknife, NT X1A 2L9

Cournoyer, Yvan
former hockey player
c/o Brasserie 12
625 32e av.
Lachine, PQ H8T 3G6

Coutts, Jim
Chairman,
Canadian Investment Capital Ltd.
161 Bay St., Ste. 3840
P.O. Box 610
Toronto, ON M5J 2S1

Coutu, Jean
Chairman, Le Groupe Jean Coutu (PJC) Inc.
discount pharmacy chain
530 rue Bériault
Longueuil, PQ J4G 1S8

Cowboy Junkies
country/rock band
c/o 2A, 143 West 69th St.
New York, NY 10023
U.S.A.

Cowin, "Hungry Jack"
Australia's fast-food king
100 William St.
Sydney, NSW 2011, Australia

Cranston, Toller
skater/artist
c/o IMG
1 St. Clair Ave. E., #700
Toronto, ON M4T 2V7

Crash Test Dummies
rock group
c/o 192 Spadina Ave., Ste. 508
Toronto, ON M5V 2C2

The CRB Foundation Ann Dadson, Administrative Director *supports the enhancement of Canadianism and the unity of the Jewish people*	1170 Peel St. Montreal, PQ H3B 4P2
Creighton, Douglas *journalist*/Founder, *The Toronto Sun*	c/o Paper and Pen Inc. BCE Place, 161 Bay St. P.O. Box 528 Toronto, ON M5J 2S1
Crewson, Wendy *actress*	c/o A.C.I. Talent Inc. 205 Ontario St., Rear Studio Toronto, ON M5A 2V6
Crispo, John *political economist/commentator*	1127 Mt. Pleasant Rd. Toronto, ON M4P 2M8
Crombie, David Edward former Mayor of Toronto	81 Glencairn Ave. Toronto, ON M4R 1M7
Cronenberg, David *film producer/director*	217 Avenue Rd. Toronto, ON M5R 2J3
Cronyn, Hume *actor*	63–23 Carlton St. Rego Park, NY 11374, U.S.A.
Cross, James R. former British Trade Commissioner *kidnapped by the FLQ*	The Small House Queen Katherine Rd. Lymington, Hants, England
Crouse, Lloyd Roseville Lieutenant-Governor of Nova Scotia	Government House 1451 Barrington St. Halifax, NS B3J 1Z2
Crow, John W. former Governor, Bank of Canada	c/o Bank of Canada 234 Wellington St. Ottawa, ON K1A 0G9
CTV Television Network Ltd. John Cassaday, President and CEO	250 Yonge St., 18th fl. Toronto, ON M5B 2L7
Cummings, Burton *rock singer, formerly of The Guess Who*	c/o The Agency 41 Britain St., Ste. 200 Toronto, ON M5A 1R7

D

"I have felt that quick comradeship of letters which is a very real comradeship, because it is a comradeship of thought and principal."

Woodrow Wilson

Dahl, Tracy *soprano*	c/o Zemsky-Green Ltd. 165 West 57th St. New York, NY 10019 U.S.A.
Daigle, Alexandre *hockey player*	c/o Ottawa Senators 301 Moodie Dr., Ste. 411 Nepean, ON K2H 9C4
Dale, Cynthia *actress*	c/o A.C.I. Talent Inc. 205 Ontario St., Rear Studio Toronto, ON M5A 2V6
Dale, Jennifer *actress*	c/o Oscars and Abrams 59 Berkeley St. Toronto, ON M5A 2W5
Dalglish, Peter Executive Director, Street Kids International	56 The Esplanade, Ste. 202 Toronto, ON M5E 1A7
Dalhousie University Howard C. Clark, President	Halifax, NS B3H 3J5
Danby, Ken *painter*	R.R. #4 Guelph, ON N1H 6J1
Danny Grossman Dance Company	511 Bloor St. W. Toronto, ON M4W 1J1

Dasko, Donna Anne
pollster

Environics
45 Charles St. E.
Toronto, ON M4Y 1S2

Davey, Keith
Liberal Senator from Ontario/
"The Rainmaker"

Room 217-EB
The Senate
Ottawa, ON K1A 0A4

David, Paul
Conservative Senator from
Nova Scotia

Room 275-E
The Senate
Ottawa, ON K1A 0A4

Davies, Robertson
author

c/o Massey College
4 Devonshire Place
Toronto, ON M5S 2E1

Davis, Fred
host, "Front Page Challenge"

c/o CBC–Front Page
Challenge
P.O. Box 500, Stn. A
Toronto, ON M5W 1E6

Davis, William (Bill)
former Premier of Ontario

c/o Tory Tory Deslauriers
& Binnington
P.O. Box 270
Toronto-Dominion Centre
Toronto, ON M5K 1N2

D'Cruz, Joseph R.
management expert

246 Bloor St. W.
Toronto, ON M5S 1V4

De Bané, Pierre
Liberal Senator from Quebec/
former federal Cabinet Minister

Room 182–F
The Senate
Ottawa, ON K1A 0A4

de Chastelain, Gen. John
Chief of the Defence Staff/
former Ambassador to the U.S.

CDS, NDHQ
MGen. G.R. Pearkes Bldg.
Ottawa, ON K1A 0K2

Decima Research
Allan Gregg, Chairman
polling company

1 Eglinton Ave. E.
Ste. 700
Toronto, ON M4P 3A1

Decore, Laurence G.
Alberta Liberal Leader

Opposition Leader's Office
204 Legislature Annex
Edmonton, AB T5K 1E4

de Cotret, Robert
Canadian representative to the World Bank/former federal Conservative Cabinet Minister from Ontario

c/o The World Bank
1818 H St., N.W.
Washington, DC 20433
U.S.A

de Havilland Inc.
Ken Laver, President

Boeing Canada
Garratt Blvd.
Downsview, ON M3K 1Y5

de Larochellière, Luc
rock singer/guitarist

C.P. 1953, Place d'Armes
Montreal, PQ H2Y 3L9

de Lint, Charles
fantasy writer/author

64 Willard St.
Ottawa, ON K15 1T8

Demers, Rock
film producer

Productions La Fête
225 est rue Roy, Ste. 203
Montreal, PQ H2W 1M5

Dene National Office
George Erasmus, National Chief

P.O. Box 2338
Yellowknife, NT X1A 2P7

Den Hertog, Johanna
adviser to the B.C. government/ former federal NDP President

Trade and Economic
Liaison Office
999 Canada Place, Ste. 740
Vancouver, BC V6C 3E1

Deol, Monika
"MuchMusic" *host*

c/o MuchMusic
299 Queen St. W.
Toronto, ON M5V 2Z5

de Pedery-Hunt, Dora
sculptor/designer

65 Glen Rd.
Toronto, ON M4W 2V3

Derome, Bernard
Radio-Canada journalist

c/o Radio-Canada
C.P. 6000
Montreal, PQ H3C 3A8

Desbarats, Peter
journalist/educator

c/o Graduate School of Journalism
University of Western Ontario
London, ON N6A 5B7

Deschenes, Jules
former Quebec Chief Justice

4854 Côte Des Neiges
Montreal, PQ H3V 1G7

Desjardins, Richard
singer/songwriter

c/o Show-Sur
5404 av. du Parc
Montreal, PQ H2V 4G9

Desmarais, Jean-Noël
Conservative Senator from Ontario

Room 807-VB
The Senate
Ottawa, ON K1A 0A4

Desmarais, Paul
Chairman and CEO,
Power Corp. of Canada

800 Place Victoria
P.O. Box 206
Stock Exchange Tower
Montreal, PQ H4Z 1E3

Devine, Grant
former Premier of Saskatchewan

Office of the Leader of the Opposition
2405 Legislative Dr.
Regina, SK S4S 0B3

Dewar, Marion
Executive Director, Canadian Council on Children and Youth/
former Mayor of Ottawa and NDP MP

869 Rex Ave.
Ottawa, ON K2A 2P6

Deware, Mabel
Conservative Senator from New Brunswick

Room 802-VB
The Senate
Ottawa, ON K1A 0A4

Diamond, Chief Billy
Waskaganish Nation Chief/
President and CEO,
Air Creebec Inc.

P.O. Box 60
Waskaganish
James Bay, PQ J0M 1R0

Diamond, Jack
architect

2 Berkeley St., Ste. 600
Toronto, ON M5A 2W3

Diana, HRH The Princess

Kensington Palace
London W8, England

Dickinson, Terence
astronomy expert/author

P.O. Box 10
Yarker, ON K0K 3N0

Dickson, Brian
former Chief Justice,
Supreme Court of Canada

c/o Supreme Court of Canada
Wellington St.
Ottawa, ON K1A 0J1

Dill, Howard
grower of world's largest pumpkin

College Rd.
Windsor, NS B0N 2T0

Diner's Club/enRoute
Don Osvag, President
credit card company

1000 Sherbrooke Ave W.
Ste. 2200
Montreal, PQ H3A 3G4

Di Nino, Consiglio
Conservative Senator from Ontario
Room 800-VB
The Senate
Ottawa, ON K1A 0A4

Dingwall, David
federal Liberal Cabinet Minister from Nova Scotia
Room 607–CB
House of Commons
Ottawa, ON K1A 0A6

Dion, Céline
popular singer
700–3100 LaCarrefour
Laval, PQ H7T 2K7

Dionne Quintuplets
Annette, Yvonne and Cécile
(Emilie, Marie; deceased)
c/o Dionne Quints Museum
P.O. Box 747
North Bay, ON P1B 8J8

Discus Music World
Jerry Wipf, CEO
music retail chain
245 Montée de Liesse
St-Laurent, PQ H4T 1P5

DMR Group Inc.
Pierre Y. Ducros, Chairman, President, and CEO
information technology development consultants
2300, 1200 McGill College
Montreal, PQ H3B 4G7

D.O.A.
rock group
c/o The Agency
41 Britain St., Ste. 200
Toronto, ON M5A 1R7

Doctors Without Borders Canada/ Médecins Sans Frontières Canada
Ben Chapman,
National Office Manager
56 The Esplanade, Ste. 203
Toronto, ON M5E 1A7

Doer, Gary
Manitoba NDP Leader
Legislative Bldgs.
Winnipeg, MB R3C 0V8

Dofasco Ltd.
Paul J. Phoenix,
Chairman and CEO
nation's largest steelmaker
P.O. Box 460
1330 Burlington St. E.
Hamilton, ON L8N 3J5

Doherty, Denny
singer, Mamas and the Papas/ actor
c/o Paradise Artists
P.O. Box 1821
Ojai, CA 93024-1821
U.S.A.

Dominion of Canada Rifle Association J.D. Salloum, Executive Director	P.O. Box 11160, Stn. H Nepean, ON K2H 7T9
Domtar Inc. Jean Campeau, Chairman *pulp and paper company*	395 de Maisonneuve ouest Montreal, PQ H3A 1L6
Donald, Donald K. *concert promoter*	200–6265 Côte-de-Liesse Montreal, PQ H4T 1C3
Donato, Andy *editorial cartoonist*	c/o *The Toronto Sun* 333 King St. E. Toronto, ON M5A 1A1
The Donner Canadian Foundation R. Couchman, President *financially supports various socio-economic issues in Canada and abroad*	402–212 King St. W. Toronto, ON M5H 1K5
The Don't Tax Reading Coalition David Hunt, Co-ordinator	260 King St. E. Toronto, ON M5A 1K3
Doody, Richard J. Conservative Senator from Ontario	Room 568-S The Senate Ottawa, ON K1A 0A4
Doohan, James *Star Trek*'s "Scotty"	c/o 3800 Barham Blvd. Los Angeles, CA 90068 U.S.A.
Doré, Jean Mayor of Montreal	275, rue Notre-Dame est Ste. 206 Montreal, PQ H2Y 1C6
Doubleday Canada Ltd. Markus Wilhelm, President *book publishing firm*	105 Bond St. Toronto, ON M5B 1Y3
Double Exposure *CBC Radio comedy show*	c/o CBC P.O. Box 500, Stn. A Toronto, ON M5W 1E6
Doucet, Clive *author*	38 Muriel St. Ottawa, ON K1J 4E1
Doug and the Slugs *rock group*	P.O. Box 65400, Stn. F Vancouver, BC V5N 5P3

Dowdswell, Elizabeth Executive Director, United Nations Environmental Program (UNEP)	P.O. Box 30552 Nairobi, Kenya
Downie, Peter former host, "Man Alive" and "Midday"	P.O. Box 423 Mt. Albert, ON L0G 1M0
Drabinsky, Garth Chairman, Live Entertainment Corporation of Canada	165 Avenue Rd. Toronto, ON M5R 2H7
Drainie, Bronwyn *journalist/author*	c/o *The Globe and Mail* 444 Front St. W. Toronto, ON M5V 2S9
Drapeau, Jean former Mayor of Montreal	5700 av. des Plaines Montreal, PQ H1T 2X1
Dryden, Ken *former NHL goalie/lawyer/author*	1414 rue Lambert-Closse Montreal, PQ H3H 1N2
Ducharme, Moira Mayor of Halifax	P.O. Box 1749, 1841 Argyle Halifax, NS B3J 3A5
Ducharme, Réjean *author*	Editions Gallimard 5 rue Sebastien Paris 75007, France
Ducks Unlimited Canada *environmental group*	1190 Waverley St. Winnipeg, MB R3T 2E2
Dudek, Louis *poet*	5 Ingleside Ave. Montreal, PQ H3Z 1N4
Duerr, Al Mayor of Calgary	P.O. Box 2100, Stn. M Calgary, AB T2P 2M5
Duffy, Mike *journalist*	Nation's Capital Television Inc. 1500 Merivale Rd. Ottawa, ON K2E 6Z5
Dufour, Ghislain President, Conseil du Patronat *employer group*	606, 2075 rue University Montreal, PQ H3A 2L1
Dumas, Antoine *wildlife artist*	1100 Marguerite-Bourgeois Sillery, PQ G1S 3X9

Dumont, Yvon
Lieutenant Governor of Manitoba/
former President, Metis
National Council

Government House
10 Kennedy St.
Winnipeg, MB R3C 1S4

Dunn, Willie
Native folk singer/songwriter

1476B Heatherington Rd.
Ottawa, ON K1V 6S1

Dupuy, Michel
federal Liberal Cabinet Minister
from Quebec/former Ambassador
to the U.N. and President of CIDA

Room 230–CB
House of Commons
Ottawa, ON K1A 0A6

Durivage, Simon
Radio-Canada TV
current affairs journalist/
former host, "Le Point"

c/o Radio-Canada
C.P. 6000
succ. Centre Ville
Montreal, PQ H3C 3A8

Duschesnay, Isabelle and Paul
Olympic skating champions

50 Grimes Ch.
Aylmer, PQ G9G 1H5

Dutoit, Charles E.
conductor

85 Ste-Catherine ouest,
Ste. 900
Montreal, PQ H2X 3P4

Dye, Kenneth M.
former federal Auditor General

1575 Esquimalt, Ste. 505
West Vancouver, BC V7V 1R4

Dying With Dignity
Marilynne Seguin,
Executive Director

600 Eglinton Ave., Ste. 401
Toronto, ON M4P 1P3

Dylex Ltd.
Wilfred Murray Posluns,
Chairman and CEO

637 Lakeshore Blvd. W.
Toronto, ON M5V 1A8

E

"A grand letter from you yesterday was like a fragrant scent in a dismal world."

Harold J. Laski

Eagleson, R. Alan founder and former Executive Director, NHL Players' Association	37 Maitland St. Toronto, ON M4Y 1C8
Earth Day Canada Robin Jones Martin, Executive Director	144 Front St. W. Ste. 250 Toronto, ON M5J 2L7
T. Eaton Co. Ltd. George Ross Eaton, President	1 Dundas St. W. Toronto, ON M5B 1C8
Eayrs, James *historian*	23 Ellis Park Rd. Toronto, ON M6S 2V4
Edmonton Eskimos Football Club Hugh Campbell, General Manager	9021–111 Ave. Edmonton, AB T5B 0C3
Edmonton Journal Linda Hughes, Publisher	P.O. Box 2421 Edmonton, AB T5J 2S6
Edmonton Oilers Hockey Club Glen Sather, General Manager	Northlands Coliseum 7424–118 St. Edmonton, AB T2B 4M9
Edmonton Space and Science Centre Les Young, Executive Director	11211–142 St. N.W. Edmonton, AB T5M 4A1
Edmonton Sun Ron Mitchell, Publisher	4990–92 Ave., Ste. 250 Edmonton, AB T6B 3A1

Edward, HRH The Prince
Buckingham Palace
London SW1, England

Edwards, Paul
Manitoba Liberal Leader
140 Roslyn Rd.
Winnipeg, MB R3L 0G8

Eggleton, Arthur
federal Liberal Cabinet Minister from Ontario/former Mayor of Toronto
Room 209–CB
House of Commons
Ottawa, ON K1A 0A6

Egoyan, Atom
film director
102, 490 Adelaide St. W.
Toronto, ON M5V 1T3

Ehm, Erica
"MuchMusic" VJ/*songwriter*
299 Queen St. W.
Toronto, ON M5V 2Z5

Eisler, Lloyd
figure skating champion
c/o IMG, 22 East 71st St.
New York, NY 10021, U.S.A.

Ekho, Jimmy
The "Arctic Elvis"/Inuit folk singer
Iqaluit, NT X0A 0H0

Elections Canada
Jean-Pierre Kingsley, Chief Electoral Officer
1595 Telesat Court
Ottawa, ON K1A 0M6

Elizabeth II, Queen
Buckingham Palace
London SW1, England

Elizabeth, Queen
The Queen Mother
Clarence House, St. James
London SW1, England

Elvis in Canada Fan Club
Frances M. Roberts, President
Lockbox #20236
Upper James Postal Stn.
Hamilton, ON L9C 7M8

Emergency Preparedness Canada
Eric Shipley, Executive Director
plans for civil emergencies
Jackson Bldg.
122 Bank St.
Ottawa, ON K1A 0W6

Encyclopaedia Britannica Publications Ltd.
David F. Durnan, President
175 Holiday Dr.
Cambridge, ON N3C 3N4

Engel, Howard
author/playwright/creator of Benny Cooperman, Canada's best-known fictional detective
281 Major St.
Toronto, ON M5S 2L5

Enright, Michael
host, CBC Radio's
"As It Happens"

c/o CBC–As It Happens
P.O. Box 500, Stn. A
Toronto, ON M5W 1E6

Environics Research Group Ltd.
Michael Adams, President
polling firm

45 Charles St. E., Ste. 200
Toronto, ON M4Y 1S2

Epp, Jake
former Conservative Cabinet
Minister from Manitoba/
Vice-President, Trans Canada
Pipelines Ltd.

P.O. Box 1000, Stn. M
Calgary, AB T2P 4K5

Epstein, William
United Nations official

UNITAR, United Nations
400 East 58th St.
New York, NY 10022, U.S.A.

Equality Party
Keith Henderson, Leader
Quebec English-rights party

#801, 5250 Ferrier
Montreal, PQ H4P 1L4

***Equinox* magazine**
Fred Laflamme, Publisher

7 Queen Victoria Rd.
Camden East, ON K0K 1J0

Erasmus, Georges
former Chief, Assembly of
First Nations

P.O. Box 222
Yellowknife, NT X1A 2N2

Erickson, Arthur
architect

2412 Laurel
Vancouver, BC V5Z 3T2

Erola, Judy
President, Pharmaceutical
Manufacturers Association of
Canada/former federal Liberal
Cabinet Minister from Ontario

11 Lewis St.
Ottawa, ON K2P 0S2

Esaw, Johnny
CTV sports broadcaster

250 Yonge St., 18th fl.
Toronto, ON M5B 2L7

**Esperanto Association
of Canada**
Wallace G. du Temple, President
international language promoter

P.O. Box 2159
Sidney, BC V8L 3S6

Esposito, Phil
owner, Tampa Bay Lightning
former hockey player

501 Kennedy Blvd.
Tampa, FL 33606
U.S.A.

Estey, Willard "Bud"
former Justice, Supreme Court of Canada

McCarthy Tetrault
Ste. 4700, T-D Bank Tower
Toronto-Dominion Centre
Toronto, ON M5K 1E6

Etrog, Sorel
sculptor/designer of the Genie award statuette

Box 5943, Stn. A
Toronto, ON M5W 1P3

Evaluardjuk, Henry
Inuit sculptor

Cape Dorset, NT X0A 0C0

Evangelista, Linda
supermodel

c/o Elite
111 East 22nd St.
New York, NY 10010
U.S.A.

Everett, Douglas
Liberal Independent Senator from Manitoba

Room 379-S
The Senate
Ottawa, ON K1A 0A4

Ewen, Paterson
artist

1015 Wellington St.
London, ON N6A 3T5

Export Development Corporation
Paul Labbé, President and CEO
federal agency that assists and promotes Canadian exports

151 O'Connor St.
Ottawa, ON K1A 1K2

Eyton, John Trevor
Conservative Senator from Ontario/
President and CEO, Brascan Ltd.

P.O. 762, BCE Place
181 Bay St.
Toronto, ON M5J 2T3

F

"A letter does not blush."

Cicero

Fairbairn, Bruce *record producer*	2744 W. 33rd Ave. Vancouver, BC V6N 2G1
Fairbairn, Joyce Liberal Senator from Alberta and Government Leader in the Senate	Room 557-S The Senate Ottawa, ON K1A 0A4
Fairclough, Ellen Louks *first female federal Cabinet Minister (1957)*	25 Stanley Ave. Hamilton, ON L8P 2K9
Fairweather, Gordon former Conservative MP from New Brunswick/*federal civil servant*	71 Somerset St. W., #1802 Ottawa, ON K2P 2G2
Falconbridge Ltd. Franklin G.T. Pickard, President and CEO *mining company*	P.O. Box 40 Commerce Court W. Toronto, ON M5L 1B4
Fallis, Mary Lou *soprano*	c/o Great World Artists Management Inc. 66 Gerrard St. E. Toronto, ON M3B 1G3
Faludy, George *poet*	Deres utca 10/B Budapest XII 1124, Hungary

Family Service Canada
Trevor Williams, President
promotes families as the primary source of nurturing and development

55 Parkdale Ave.
Ottawa, ON K1Y 4G1

Famous People Players
Diane Dupuy, Creator and President
black-light puppet troupe

45 Lisgar St.
Toronto, ON M6J 3T3

Fantasy Balloon Owners and Pilots Association
Karen Rosenthal, Director
hot air ballooning awareness organization

205 Bridge St.
New Dundee, ON N0B 2E0

Farnon, Robert J.
conductor/musician

La Falaise
St. Martin's, Guernsey
Channel Islands

Farquharson, Charlie
TV character/author

125 Dupont St.
Toronto, ON M5R 1V4

Farquharson, Right Rev. Walter
former Moderator,
United Church of Canada

P.O. Box 126
Saltcoats, SK S0A 3R0

Faulkner, Hugh
former federal Liberal Cabinet Minister from Quebec/Executive Director, Business Council on Sustainable Development (Geneva)

157 Cap St-Jacques
Pierrefonds, PQ H9K 1C4

Fecan, Ivan
V.P., Baton Broadcasting Inc.
TV producer

Baton Broadcasting Inc.
P.O. Box 9, Stn. O
Toronto, ON M4A 2M9

Federal Business Development Bank (FBDB)
Bertrand J. Lavoie, Chairman

P.O. Box 335
Stock Exchange Station
Montreal, PQ H4Z 1L4

Federation of Sikh Societies of Canada
Mohinder Singh Gosal, President

P.O. Box 91, Stn. B
Ottawa, ON K1P 6C3

Fedoruk, Sylvia
Lieutenant Governor of Saskatchewan
Government House
4607 Dewdney Ave.
Regina, SK S4P 3V7

Feldbrill, Victor
conductor
170 Hillhurst Blvd.
Toronto, ON M5N 1P2

Ferguson, Ivan
inventor of the IMAX and OMNIMAX movie screens
IMAX Space Technology Inc.
45 Charles St. E.
Toronto, ON M4Y 1S2

Ferguson, John
former hockey player/hockey executive
c/o Ottawa Senators
411–301 Moodie Dr.
Nepean, ON K2H 9C4

Ferguson, Maynard
world-renowned trumpet player
c/o P.O. Box 716
Ojai, CA 93023 U.S.A.

Ferguson, Trevor
author
3463 rue Walkely
Montreal, PQ H4B 2K2

Festival des Films du Monde
Serge Losique, President
international film festival
1455 de Maisonneuve ouest
Ste. 109
Montreal, PQ H3G 1M8

Festival "Juste Pour Rire" Just for Laughs
Gilbert Rozon, President
301 de Maisonneuve est
Montreal, PQ H2X 1K1

Fielding, Joy
author
c/o Stoddart Canada
34 Lesmill Rd.
Don Mills, ON M3B 2T6

54/40
rock band
c/o Gangland Artists
810 W. Broadway Ave., Ste. 707
Vancouver, BC V5Z 1J8

Figgy Duff
folk band
13 Power St.
St. John's, NF A1E 1K6

Filmon, Gary
Premier of Manitoba
Room 204
Legislative Building
Winnipeg, MB R3C 0V8

Financial Post
Douglas Knight, Publisher
333 King St. E.
Toronto, ON M5A 4N2

Findley, Timothy
author
P.O. Box 419
Cannington, ON L0E 1E0

Finn, D'Arcy
founding Director, Canadian
Security Intelligence Service

c/o Office of the Deputy
Minister, DND
101 Colonel By Dr.
Ottawa, ON K1A 0K2

Finn, Gilbert
Lieutenant-Governor of
New Brunswick

P.O. Box 6000
Fredericton, NB E3B 5H1

Finnigan, Joan
author

Hartington, ON K0H 1W0

Fiset, Edouard
chief architect of Expo 67

600–1980 Sherbrooke W.
Montreal, PQ H3H 1E8

Fisher, Douglas
political columnist/commentator

c/o Parliamentary Press Gallery
Ottawa, ON K1A 0A8

***Flare* magazine**
Shelly M. Black, Editor
Canada's fashion magazine

777 Bay St.
Toronto, ON M5W 1A7

Fogh, Hans
sailmaker/competitive yachtsman

2242 Lakeshore Blvd. W.
Toronto, ON M8V 1A5

Fontaine, Phil
Manitoba Grand Chief

400–286 Smith St.
Winnipeg, MB R3C 1K4

Forbes, Roy (Bim)
folk singer/songwriter

932 Semlin Dr.
Vancouver, BC V5L 4J8

Ford, Glen
actor

9200 Sunset Blvd., #318
Los Angeles, CA 90069
U.S.A.

Ford, Robert A.D.
former diplomat/poet

La Poivrière
St-Sylvestre-Pragoulin
63310 Randan, France

Ford Motor Company of Canada
Kenneth W. Harrigan,
Chairman and CEO

The Canadian Rd.
Oakville, ON L6J 5E4

Forde, Leneen
first female Governor of
Australia's Queensland State

Government House
Fernberg Rd., Paddington
Queensland 4064, Australia

Forrestal, Thomas D. "Tom"
artist

3 Albert St.
Dartmouth, NS B2Y 3M1

Forrestall, J. Michael
Conservative Senator from
Nova Scotia/former MP

Room 154-N
The Senate
Ottawa, ON K1A 0A4

Forrester, Maureen
contralto

c/o Harold Shaw
1900 Broadway, 2nd fl.
New York, NY 10023 U.S.A.

Forrestier, Louise
singer

c/o Spectra Scene
355 Ste-Catherine ouest, Ste. 700
Montreal, PQ H3B 1A5

Forst, Judith
mezzo-soprano

428 Princeton Ave.
Port Moody, BC V3H 3L3

Fortier, d'Iberville
former Official Languages
Commissioner

29 Mackinnon St.
Rockcliffe Park
Ottawa, ON K1M 0G4

Fortier, L. Yves
former Ambassador to UN

c/o Ogilvy Renault
1981 McGill College Ave.
Ste. 1100
Montreal, PQ H3A 3C1

Fortress Louisbourg
Anne O'Neil, Chief of
Visitor Services

P.O. Box 160
Louisbourg, NS B0A 1M0

Forum for Young Canadians

801–251 Laurier Ave. W.
Ottawa, ON K1P 5J6

Foster, David
composer/songwriter

435–3575 Cahuenga Blvd. W.
Los Angeles, CA 90068
U.S.A.

Fotheringham, Allan
journalist/"Front Page Challenge" panellist

c/o *Maclean's*, 777 Bay St.
Toronto, ON M5W 1A7

Four Seasons Hotel Inc.
Isadore Sharp, Chairman,
President, and CEO

1165 Leslie St.
Don Mills, ON M3C 2K8

Fowke, Edith
folklorist

5 Notley Place
Toronto, ON M4B 2M7

Fox, Francis
former federal Liberal
Cabinet Minister from Quebec

P.O. Box 242
800 Victoria Sq., Ste 3400
Montreal, PQ H4Z 1E9

Fox, George
country musician
c/o Balmur Ltd.
4950 Yonge St., Ste. 2400
Toronto, ON M2N 6K1

Fox, Michael J.
actor
16030 Bentara Blvd., Ste. 380
Encino, CA 91436, U.S.A.

Foxcroft, Ron
FOX40 whistle creator
c/o Fortron Int'l. Inc.
20 Warrington St.
Hamilton, ON L8E 3V1

Franca, Celia
ballerina/choreographer/ ballet director
250 Clemow Ave.
Ottawa, ON K1S 2B6

***Frank* magazine**
Michael Bate, Editor
P.O. Box 2462, Stn. D
Ottawa, ON K1P 5W6

Frappier, Roger
film producer
c/o Max Films Inc.
5130 boul. St-Laurent, 4e
Montreal, PQ H2T 1R8

Fraser, Brad
playwright
11605 97 St.
Edmonton, AB T5G 1Y1

Fraser, Duncan
writer
Grand Pré
Kings Co., NS B0P 1M0

Fraser, Graham
Ottawa Bureau Chief, *The Globe and Mail*
165 Sparks St., 3rd fl.
Ottawa, ON K1P 5B9

Fraser, John
Ambassador for the Environment/ former House of Commons Speaker
1948 West 15th Ave.
Vancouver, BC V6J 2L3

Fraser Institute
Michael Walker, Executive Director
Conservative think tank
626 Bute St., 2nd fl.
Vancouver, BC V6E 3M1

Frechette, Louise
Ambassador to UN
866 United Nations Plaza, #250
New York, NY 10017-1897
U.S.A.

Frechette, Sylvie
synchronized swimmer, Olympic gold medallist
c/o Daniel Lamarre
National Public Relations
1600–770 Sherbrooke St. W.
Montreal, PQ H3A 1G1

Free Methodist Church in Canada
Donald N. Bastian, President
4315 Village Centre Court
Mississauga, ON L4Z 1S2

Freedman, Harry
composer
35 St. Andrews Gardens
Toronto, ON M4W 2C9

Freschi, Bruno Basilio
architect
166 Cleveland Ave.
Buffalo, NY 14222, U.S.A.

Frewer, Matt
actor/"Max Headroom"
9200 Sunset Blvd., #625
Los Angeles, CA 90069 U.S.A.

Friendly Giant
(Bob Homme)
children's TV character
P.O. Box 137
Grafton, ON K0K 2G0

The Friends of Breastfeeding Society
Catherine Young, Chairmother
R.R. #2
Chesley, ON N0G 1L0

Friends of Canadian Broadcasting
Ian Morrison, Steering Committee Head
29 Prince Arthur Ave.
Toronto, ON M5R 1B2

Friends of the Earth
Susan Tanner, Executive Director
#701, 251 Laurier Ave. W.
Ottawa, ON K1P 5J6

Frith, Royce
Liberal Senator from Ontario
Room 371-S, The Senate
Ottawa, ON K1A 0A4

Front Page Challenge
TV quiz show
P.O. Box 500, Stn. A
Toronto, ON M5W 1E6

Frozen Ghost
rock band
15–155 Toryork Dr.
Weston, ON M9L 1X9

Fulford, Robert
author/writer
19 Lynwood Ave.
Toronto, ON M4V 1K3

Fulton, Davie
former federal Conservative Cabinet Minister from B.C.
1632 West 40th Ave.
Vancouver, BC V6M 1V9

Fur Council of Canada
Del Haylock, Executive Director
1435 St-Alexander, #1270
Montreal, PQ H3A 2G4

G

"Carrier of news and knowledge,
Instrument of trade and industry,
Promoter of mutual acquaintance,
Of peace and good-will
Among men and nations."

Inscription on Post Office, Washington, D.C.
by Charles W. Eliot

Gabereau, Vicki
host, CBC Radio's "Gabereau"
c/o CBC
P.O. Box 4600
Vancouver, BC V6B 4A2

Gable, Brian
editorial cartoonist
c/o *The Globe and Mail*
444 Front St. W.
Toronto, ON M5V 2S9

Gabriel, Tony
former CFL football player
c/o Ottawa Rough Riders
Lansdowne Park
Ottawa, ON K1S 3W7

Gagnon, André
composer/pianist
2686 Laval St.
Montreal, PQ H2X 3C9

Gagnon, André-Philippe
comedian
89 Alexandra St.
Granby, PQ J2G 2P4

Gagnon, Lysiane
journalist
c/o *La Presse*
7 rue St-Jacques
Montreal, PQ H2Y 1K9

Galbraith, John Kenneth
economist
Harvard University
207 Littauer Center
Cambridge, MA 02138
U.S.A.

Galdikas, Dr. Birute *world's foremost expert on orangutans*	Orangutan Foundation International 822 South Wellesley Ave. Los Angeles, CA 90049, U.S.A.
Gallant, Mavis *author*	14 rue Jean Ferrandi Paris 75006, France
Galloway, Jim *saxophonist*	204A George St. Toronto, ON M5R 2N6
Gallup Canada Inc. John C. Wood, President and CEO *polling firm*	180 Bloor St. W. Toronto, ON M5S 2V6
Ganong, David Alison Chairman, Ganong Bros. Ltd. *chocolate manufacturer*	One Chocolate Dr. St. Stephen, NB E3L 2X5
Garneau, Capt. Marc *first Canadian astronaut*	Canadian Astronaut Program Canadian Space Agency P.O. Box 7014, Stn. V Vanier, ON K1L 8E2
Garner, David Emmett *actor/director*	25381 Kennedy Rd. R.R. #1 Sutton West, ON L0E 1R0
Gartner, Hana *co-host, CBC's "the 5th estate"*	c/o CBC–the 5th estate P.O. Box 500, Stn. A Toronto, ON M5W 1E6
Gaudaur, Jake "Mr. CFL"/former CFL Commissioner	3082 Balmoral Ave. Burlington, ON L7N 1E4
The Gazette Joan Fraser, Editor-in-Chief	250 St. Antoine St. W. Montreal, PQ H2Y 3R7
Geddes, Gary *author/playwright*	R.R. #1 Dunvegan, ON K0C 1J0
Gehry, Frank *architect/designer*	1520-B Cloverfield Blvd. Santa Monica, CA 90404-3543 U.S.A.
Gelinas, Gratien *author/"Ti-Coc" creator*	Box 207, 316 Girouard St. Oka, PQ J0N 1E0

General Motors of Canada Ltd. George Peapples, President	1908 Colonel Sam Dr. Oshawa, ON L1H 8P7
Genovese, Nick *blind former national golfing champion*	138 Little John Rd. Dundas, ON L9H 4H3
George, Leonard Chief, Burrard Band of the Coast Salish/*son of Chief Dan George*	3082 Ghum-Iye Dr. North Vancouver, BC V7H 1B3
George, Vice Admiral Robert E. Commander, Maritime Command, Canadian Navy	MARCOM HQ, FMO Halifax, NS B3K 2X0
Ghauri, Yasmine *supermodel*	c/o Giovanni Model Mgmt. 291 Place d'Youville Montreal, PQ H2Y 2B5
Ghermezian Brothers (Bahman, Eskander, Nader, and Raphael) *owners of the West Edmonton Mall/real estate developers*	c/o Triple Five Corp. Ltd. 900–9707 110 St. N.W. Edmonton, AB T5K 2L9
Gherson, Giles *journalist*	c/o *The Globe and Mail* 444 Front St. W. Toronto, ON M5V 2S9
Getty, Donald R. former Premier of Alberta	Legislative Building Edmonton, AB T5K 2B6
Ghitter, Ronald Conservative Senator from Alberta	Room 901-VB The Senate Ottawa, ON K1A 0A4
Ghiz, Joseph former Premier of P.E.I. *law school dean*	Dalhousie Law School Weldon Law Bldg. 6061 University Ave. Halifax, NS B3H 3J5
Giannou, Dr. Chris *war surgeon*	c/o Janetos 1 Revlis Cres. Scarborough, ON M1V 1E8
Gibson, Graeme *author*	c/o The Writers' Union of Canada 24 Ryerson Ave. Toronto, ON M5T 2P3

Gibson, William
author

c/o Fitzhenry & Whiteside
195 Allstate Pkwy.
Markham, ON L3R 4T8

Gigantés, Philippe D.
Liberal Senator from Ontario

Room 202-VB
The Senate
Ottawa, ON K1A 0A4

Gillespie, Alastair
former federal Liberal Cabinet Minister from Ontario

175 Heath St. W.
Toronto, ON M4V 1V1

Gilmour, Clyde
host, CBC Radio's "Gilmour's Albums"

c/o CBC–Gilmour's Albums
P.O. Box 500, Stn. A
Toronto, ON M5W 1E6

Gilmour, David
author/broadcaster

c/o CBC-Prime Time News
P.O. Box 14000, Stn. A
Toronto, ON M5B 1Y2

Gilmour, Doug
hockey player

c/o Toronto Maple Leafs
60 Carlton St.
Toronto, ON M5B 1L1

Girl Guides of Canada
Marsha Ross,
Chief Commissioner

50 Merton St.
Toronto, ON M4S 1A3

Glass, Joanna M.
playwright

c/o Playwrights Union of Canada
54 Wolseley St., 2nd fl.
Toronto, ON M5C 1A5

Glass Tiger
rock band

14 Sumach St.
Toronto, ON M5A 3J4

Glenbow Museum
Dr. Robert Janes, Director

130 9th Ave. S.E.
Calgary, AB T2G 0P3

Global Television Network
James F. Sward, CEO

81 Barber Greene Rd.
Don Mills, ON M3C 2A2

The Globe and Mail
William Greenhalgh,
President and Publisher

444 Front St. W.
Toronto, ON M5V 2S9

Godfrey, Paul
CEO, Toronto Sun Publishing Corp.

333 King St. E.
Toronto, ON M5A 3X5

Goldbloom, Victor Commissioner of Official Languages	110 O'Connor St. 14th fl. Ottawa, ON K1A 0T8
Goldchain, Rafael *photographer*	175 Bain Ave. Toronto, ON M4K 1E9
Goldfarb, Martin *pollster*	The Goldfarb Group 4950 Yonge St., Ste. 1700 Toronto, ON M2N 6K1
Gonthier, Charles Justice, Supreme Court of Canada	Supreme Court of Canada Wellington St. Ottawa, ON K1A 0J1
The Good Brothers *country singers*	c/o Savannah Music Group 5509 Eglinton Ave. W., Ste. 207 Etobicoke, ON M9C 5K6
Goodale, Ralph federal Liberal Cabinet Minister from Saskatchewan/former provincial Liberal Leader	Room 175–EB House of Commons Ottawa, ON K1A 0A6
Goodyear, Scott *race car driver*	P.O. Box 21544 Upper Canada Outlet Newmarket, ON L3Y 8J1
Gotlieb, Allan E. former Ambassador to U.S. *political consultant*	Burston-Marsteller Canada 80 Bloor St. W., Ste 1400 Toronto, ON M5S 2V1
Gotlieb, Sondra *author/columnist*	c/o Writers' Union of Canada 24 Ryerson Ave. Toronto, ON M5T 2P3
Gould, Allan *writer/broadcaster*	31 Glen Rush Blvd. Toronto, ON M5N 2T4
Goulet, Robert *singer/actor*	c/o Rogo & Rove 2700 E. Sunset Rd., Ste. C-27 Las Vegas, NV 89120 U.S.A.
Gowan, Lawrence *rock singer*	c/o S.R.O. Productions. 189 Carlton St. Toronto, ON M5A 2K7

Grafstein, Jerahmiel
Liberal Senator from Ontario

Room 214–EB
The Senate
Ottawa, ON K1A 0A4

Graham, Alasdair
Liberal Senator from Nova Scotia

Room 264-EB
The Senate
Ottawa, ON K1A 0A4

Granatstein, Jack L.
historian/author

History Dept.
York University
4700 Keele St.
North York, ON M3J 1P3

Grand Orange Lodge of Canada (British America)
Norman R. Ritchie,
Grand Secretary

94 Sheppard Ave. W.
Willowdale, ON M2N 1M5

Grandparents Requesting Access and Dignity Society (GRAND Society)
Joan Brooks

601–20 Shallmar Blvd.
Toronto, ON M5N 1J5

Les Grands Ballets Canadiens
Lawrence Rhodes,
Artistic Director

4816 Rivard
Montreal, PQ H2J 2N6

Grant, Ted
photographer

1817 Feltham Rd.
Victoria, BC V8N 2A4

Grapes of Wrath
rock group

Box 330, 1755 Robson St.
Vancouver, BC V6G 3B7

Gratton, Michael
journalist/former Prime Ministerial aide

c/o *The Ottawa Sun*
380 Hunt Club Rd.
Ottawa, ON K1G 5H7

Gray, Charlotte
political columnist

183 Mackay St.
Ottawa, ON K1M 2B5

Gray, Herb
federal Liberal Cabinet Minister from Ontario

Room 209-S
House of Commons
Ottawa, ON K1A 0A6

Gray, John
journalist

c/o *The Globe and Mail*
444 Front St.
Toronto, ON M5V 2S9

Gray, John Howard
playwright/composer/satirist/director
3392 West 37th Ave.
Vancouver, BC V6N 2V6

Grealis, Walt
"Godfather of Canadian Content"/founder and Editor, *R.P.M.* magazine
6 Brentcliffe Rd.
Toronto, ON M4G 3Y2

Green Party of Canada
Chris Lea, Leader
831 Commercial Dr.
Vancouver, BC V5L 3W6

Greene, Graham
actor
c/o Gary Goddard & Assoc.
501 Yonge St., Ste. 208
Toronto, ON M4Y 1Y4

Greene-Raine, Nancy
Olympic gold medal skier
P.O. Box 418
Whistler, BC V0N 1B0

Greenpeace Canada
Michael Manolson, Executive Director
185 Spadina Ave., Ste. 600
Toronto, ON M5T 2C6

Greenspan, Edward
criminal lawyer
c/o Greenspan, Rosenberg and Buhr
401 Bay St., 32nd fl.
Toronto, ON M5H 2Y4

Gretzky, Wayne
hockey player
c/o Los Angeles Kings
P.O. Box 17013
Inglewood, CA 90308, U.S.A.

Greyhound Lines of Canada Ltd.
Dick Huisman, President and CEO
877 Greyhound Way S.W.
Calgary, AB T3C 3V8

Grimard, Normand
Conservative Senator from Quebec
Room 201–S
The Senate
Ottawa, ON K1A 0A4

Gros-Louis, Magella (Max)
Chief, Huron-Wendat Nation
255 Place Chef Michel Laveau
Wendake, PQ G0A 4V0

Groupe Vidéotron ltée.
André Chagnon, Chairman of the Board and CEO
leader in television of the future
2000 rue Berri
Montreal, PQ H2L 4V7

Gruben, Roger
Native business leader
Inuvialuit Regional Corp.
P.O. Box 2120
Inuvik, NT X0E 0T0

Gulf Canada Resources Ltd.
C.E. Shultz, President and CEO
P.O. Box 130
Calgary, AB T2P 2H7

Gustafson, Leonard
Conservative Senator/former Conservative MP from Saskatchewan
Room 603-VB
The Senate
Ottawa, ON K1A 0A4

Gustafson, Ralph
poet
North Hatley, PQ J0B 2C0

Guy Lombardo Music Centre and Museum
Ron Shadbolt, Managing Director
205 Wonderland Rd. S.
London, ON N6K 3T3

Gwyn, Richard
journalist/author
300 Carlton St.
Toronto, ON M5A 2L5

Gwyn, Sandra
journalist/author
300 Carlton St.
Toronto, ON M5A 2L5

Gzowski, Peter
host, CBC Radio's "Morningside"
c/o CBC–Morningside
P.O. Box 500, Stn. A
Toronto, ON M5W 1E6

H

"The best letters of our times are those that can never be published."

Virginia Woolf

Haidasz, Stanley Liberal Senator from Ontario	Room 215-EB The Senate Ottawa, ON K1A 0A4
Haig, Don *film and TV producer*	c/o Film Artists 424 Adelaide St. E. Toronto, ON M5A 1N4
Hailey, Arthur *author*	c/o Lyford Cay P.O. Box N-7776 Nassau, Bahamas
Hall, Emmett "father of medicare" *in Canada*	620 Spadina Cres. Ste. 1205 Saskatoon, SK S7K 3T5
Hall, Monty "Let's Make a Deal" host *TV producer*	Monty Hall Enterprises 519 North Arden Dr. Beverly Hills, CA 90210 U.S.A.
Halstead, John G.H. *international affairs expert/ former diplomat*	187 Billings Ave. Ottawa, ON K1H 5K8
Halton, David senior Washington correspondent, CBC TV News	5070 Macomb St., N.W. Washington, DC 20016 U.S.A.
Hamel, Jean-Marc former Chief Electoral Officer	2376 Wyndale Cres. Ottawa, ON K1H 7A6

Hamilton, Alvin
former federal Conservative
Cabinet Minister from Ontario

4 Kitoman Cres.
Manotick, ON K0A 2N0

Hamilton, Linda
actress

c/o 10100 Santa Monica Blvd.
#1600
Los Angeles, CA 90067, U.S.A.

Hamilton Tiger Cats
Football Club
John Gregory, Head Coach

75 Balsam Ave. N.
Hamilton, ON L8L 8C1

Hanomansing, Ian
CBC journalist

c/o CBC Vancouver
P.O. Box 4600
Vancouver, BC V6B 4A2

Hansen, Rick
"Man in Motion"/*physically disabled spokesperson*

The Rick Hansen National
Fellow Programme
University of British Columbia
Disability Resource Centre
1896 East Mall
Vancouver, BC V6T 1Z1

Harcourt, Mike
Premier of British Columbia

The Premier's Office
Legislative Building
Victoria, BC V8V 1X4

Hardy, Hagood
pianist/composer

277 Lakeshore Rd. E.
Oakville, ON L6J 1H9

Harkness, Douglas S.
former Federal Conservative
Cabinet Minister

716 Imperial Way S.W.
Calgary, AB T2S 1N7

Harlequin
rock group

c/o Hungry I Agency
2025 Corydon Ave., #207
Winnipeg, MB R3P 0N4

Harlequin Enterprises Ltd.
Brian Hickey, President and CEO
world's largest romance novel publisher

225 Duncan Mill Rd.
Don Mills, ON M3B 3K9

Harnoy, Ofra
cellist

122 Alfred Ave.
Willowdale, ON M2N 3H9

Harper, Elijah
Liberal MP from Manitoba/*former provincial NDP politician who helped defeat Meech Lake accord*
House of Commons
Room 331–CB
Ottawa, ON K1A 0A6

Harris, Jack
Newfoundland NDP Leader
Confederation Bldg.
P.O. Box 8700
St. John's, NF A1B 4J6

Harris, Marjorie
author
199 Albany Ave.
Toronto, ON M5R 3C7

Harris, Michael T.
writer/TV news director
P.O. Box 2020, NTV
St. John's, NF A1C 5S2

Harris, Michael T.
Ontario Conservative Party Leader
Room 116, Mowat Block
Queen's Park
Toronto, ON M7A 1A2

Harrison, Ted
artist
2029 Romney Place
Victoria, BC V85 4J6

Harron, Don
(Charlie Farquharson)
author/comical social observer
261 Davenport Rd., Ste. 301
Toronto, ON M5R 1K3

Harrop, Graham
"Back Bench" *cartoonist*
1812 Greer Ave., Apt. 212
Vancouver, BC V6J 1C5

***Harrowsmith* magazine**
Michael Webster, Editor
7 Queen Victoria Rd.
Camden East, ON K0K 1J0

Hart, Corey
rock singer
c/o Hart-Line
P.O. Box 1100, Stn. A
Montreal, PQ H3C 2X6

Hart, Evelyn
ballerina
c/o Royal Winnipeg Ballet
380 Graham Ave.
Winnipeg, MB R3C 4K2

Hartt, Stanley
Chairman, CAMDEV Corp.
former federal civil servant
40 King St. W.
Ste. 5800
Toronto, ON M5H 3Y8

Harwood, Vanessa Claire
ballerina
c/o The National Ballet of Canada
157 King St. E.
Toronto, ON M5C 1G9

Haslam, Phyllis George
social worker
13 Washington Ave.
Toronto, ON M5S 1L1

Hastings, Earl Liberal Senator from Alberta	Room 225-EB The Senate Ottawa, ON K1A 0A4
Hawkins, "Rompin" Ronnie *country singer*	c/o Backstage Productions International 3015 Kennedy Rd., Ste. 1 Scarborough, ON M1V 1E7
Hayes, Eric *photographer*	Jordan Falls, NS B0T 1J0
Hays, Daniel Liberal Senator from Alberta	Room 363-E The Senate Ottawa, ON K1A 0A4
Head, Ivan L. former president, International Development Research Centre	Faculty of Law University of British Columbia 1822 East Mall Vancouver, BC V6T 1Z1
Hébert, Anne *author*	24 rue de Pontoise Paris 75005, France
Hébert, Jacques Liberal Senator from Quebec *founder of Katimavik*	Room 374-F The Senate Ottawa, ON K1A 0A4
Hees, George Harris former federal Conservative Cabinet Minister from Ontario	7 Coltrin Place Rockliffe Park Ottawa, ON K1M 0A5
H.J. Heinz Co. of Canada Ltd. Thomas D. Smyth, Chairman	5650 Yonge St., 16th fl. Toronto, ON M2M 4G3
Helfer, Tricia *supermodel*	c/o Ford Model Agency 344 E. 59th St. New York, NY 10022, U.S.A.
Helix *hard rock band*	P.O. Box 515 Waterloo, ON N2J 4A9
Hellstrom, Brig. Gen. Sheila A. *first woman general in Canadian Armed Forces*	2048 Valley Dr. Ottawa, ON K1G 2P4
Hellyer, Paul former federal Liberal Cabinet Minister from Ontario	65 Harbour Square Ste. 506 Toronto, ON M5J 2L4

Henderson, Paul
former hockey player

c/o Maple Leaf Gardens
60 Carlton St.
Toronto, ON M5B 1L1

Henning, Doug
illusionist/V.P., Natural Law Party of Canada

c/o 11940 San Vicente Blvd.
#49032
Los Angeles, CA 90049 U.S.A.

Henriques, Richard
architect

402 W. Pender St.
Vancouver, BC V6B 1T6

Henry, Martha
stage actress

90 Mornington St.
Stratford, ON N5A 5E8

Heritage Canada
Jacques Dalibard,
Executive Director
promotes heritage conservation

306 Metcalfe St., Stn. B
Ottawa, ON K2P 1S2

Hermaniuk, Most Rev. Maxim
Archbishop Metropolitan of the Ukrainian Catholics in Canada

235 Scotia St.
Winnipeg, MB R2V 1V7

Heroux, Denis
film producer

Astral Europa
Communications, Ste. 900
2100 rue Ste-Catherine ouest
Montreal, PQ H3H 2T3

Herzberg, Dr. Gerhard
Nobel Prize-winning physicist

Herzberg Institute of Astrophysics
National Research Council
100 Sussex Dr.
Ottawa, ON K1A 0R6

Highway, Tompson
playwright

449 Shuter St.
Toronto, ON M5A 1X4

Hill, Arthur
actor

Creative Artists Agency
1888 Century Park E., Ste. 1400
Los Angeles, CA 90067
U.S.A.

Hill, Dan
rock musician

1407 Mount Pleasant Rd.
Toronto, ON M4N 2T9

Hill, Daniel G.
Ombudsman of Ontario

125 Queen's Park
Toronto, ON M5S 2C7

Hill, Tom
Native artist/Director, Woodland Indian Cultural Centre

184 Mohawk St.
Brantford, ON N3S 7G5

Hiller, Arthur *film director*/President, Directors' Guild of America	c/o Phil Gersh Agency 232 N. Canon Dr. Beverly Hills, CA 90210 U.S.A.
Hillier, James *electron microscope inventor*	22 Arreton Rd. Princeton, NJ 08540 U.S.A.
Hindle, Art *actor*	c/o CTV–E.N.G. 250 Yonge St., 18th fl. Toronto, ON M5B 2L7
Hines, Sherman *photographer*	Old Stone House R.R. #2, Newport Hants Co., NS B0N 2A0
Hiram Walker Allied Vintners Ltd. John A. Giffen, Chairman and CEO *spirits manufacturer*	P.O. Box 2518 2072 Riverside Dr. E. Windsor, ON N8Y 4S5
Hiroshima-Nagasaki Relived Setsuko Thurlow *anti-nuclear awareness group*	69 Olsen Dr. North York, ON M3A 3J4
HMV Canada Paul Alofs, President *music retail chain*	5401 Eglinton Ave. W. Ste. 110 Etobicoke, ON M9C 5K6
Hnatyshyn, Ramon J. Governor General of Canada	Government House 1 Sussex Dr. Ottawa, ON K1A 0A1
Hockey Canada Ron Robison, President	P.O. Box 1060 Calgary, AB T2P 2K8
Hockey Hall of Fame and Museum David Taylor, President	BCE Place 30 Yonge St. Toronto, ON M5E 1X8
Hockey Night in Canada Ron Harrison, Executive Producer	c/o CBC P.O. Box 500, Stn. A Toronto, ON M5W 1E6

Hodgins, Arthur
author

Dept. of Creative Writing
University of Victoria
P.O. Box 1700
Victoria, BC V8V 2Y2

Holbrook, Elizabeth Bradford
sculptor

1177 Mineral Springs Rd.
R.R. #3, Dundas, ON L9H 5E3

Holt Renfrew & Co. Ltd.
Galen Weston,
Chairman and President
retail clothing chain

22 St. Clair Ave. E.
Ste. 2001
Toronto, ON M4T 2S3

Holzman, Jacquelin
Mayor of Ottawa

111 Sussex Dr.
Ottawa, ON K1N 5A1

Homolka, Karla (Karla Teale)
convicted of manslaughter in Ontario schoolgirl slayings

c/o Prison for Women
P.O. Box 515
Kingston, ON K7L 4W7

Honda Canada Inc.
Isao Suzuki, President and CEO

715 Milner Ave.
Scarborough, ON M1B 2K8

Honeymoon Suite
rock band

41 Britain St., Ste. 200
Toronto, ON M5A 1R7

Hongkong Bank of Canada
William Dalton,
President and CEO
largest foreign bank in Canada

885 W. Georgia St.
Ste. 300
Vancouver, BC V6C 3E9

Hood, Hugh
author/writer

4242 Hampton Ave.
Montreal, PQ H4A 2K9

Hopps, Dr. John
pacemaker developer

309 1500 Riverside Dr.
Ottawa, ON K1G 4J4

Horner, Jack H.
former federal Conservative and Liberal MP

Pollockville, AB T0J 2L0

Hosek, Chaviva
Adviser to the Prime Minister/
former President, National Action Committee on the Status of Women

c/o Prime Minister's Office
80 Wellington St.
Ottawa, ON K1A 0A2

Hospital, Janette Turner
author

c/o McClelland & Stewart
481 University Ave.
Ste. 900
Toronto, ON M5G 2E9

Hotte, Jean "The King of Canadian Collectors"	Maison Jean Hotte 405 ch. de la Grande Côte St-Eustache, PQ J7P 1H7
House of Commons	Parliament Buildings Wellington St. Ottawa, ON K1A 0A6
Houston, James *author/glass designer/Inuit art promoter*	24 Main St. Stonington, CT 06378 U.S.A.
Howe, Gordie *former hockey great/* "Mr. Hockey"	32 Plank Lane Glastonbury, CT 06033 U.S.A.
Howie, Al *world class ultramarathon runner*	c/o Buenavista Beach Motel Qualicum Beach Vancouver Island, BC V9K 2C6
Hoy, Claire *journalist/author*	23 Clarendon Ave. Ottawa, ON K1Y 0P3
Hudson Institute Marie-Josée Drouin, Executive Director *economic think tank*	666 Sherbrooke St. W. Ste. 700 Montreal, PQ H3A 1E7
Hudson's Bay Company George J. Kosich, President and CEO	401 Bay St. Toronto, ON M5H 4Y4
Huggan, Isabel *author*	c/o MGA Agency 10 St. Mary St., Ste. 510 Toronto, ON M4Y 1P9
Hughes, Monica *children's author*	13816–110 Ave. Edmonton, AB T5M 2M9
Hull, Bobby *professional hockey's former* "Golden Jet"	601 Lake Hinsdale Dr. Willowbrook, IL 60514 U.S.A.
Hull, Brett *hockey player*	c/o St. Louis Blues 5700 Oakland Ave. St. Louis, MO 63110-1318, U.S.A.
Human Animal Bond Association of Canada *studies animal-human interactions*	87 Elmhurst Dr. Etobicoke, ON M9W 2J8

Human Rights Institute of Canada
Marguerite E. Ritchie,
Founder and President
303–246 Queen St.
Ottawa, ON K1P 5E4

Humanist Association of Canada
Philip Jones, President
P.O. Box 3736, Stn. C
Ottawa, ON K1Y 4J8

Humphrey, John
President, World Conference on Religion and Peace (Canadian branch) *international human rights expert*
30 Thurlow Rd., Hampstead
Montreal, PQ H3X 3G6

Humpty Dumpty Foods Ltd.
Duncan B. Cameron, President
snack food manufacturer
2100 Norman St.
Lachine, PQ H8S 1B1

Hunley, W. Helen
Alberta Lieutenant-Governor
Legislative Building
Edmonton, AB T5K 2B6

Hunter, Tommy (Thomas James)
Canada's singing "Country Gentleman"
c/o Brian Edwards
P.O. Box 1282
Peterborough, ON K9J 7H5

Hurtig, Mel
Leader, National Party of Canada
former book publisher
9905–115 St.
Edmonton, AB T5K 1S4

Husky Oil Ltd.
Arthur Price, President and CEO
P.O. Box 6525, Stn. D
Calgary, AB T2P 3G7

Hutt, William
stage actor/director
4 Waterloo St. N.
Stratford, ON N5A 5H4

Hyde, Anthony
author
c/o Penguin Books Canada
10 Alcorn Ave., Ste 300
Toronto, ON M4V 3B2

Hydro Quebec
Richard Drouin,
Chairman of the Board and CEO
75 boul. René-Lévesque ouest
Montreal, PQ H2Z 1A4

Hyundai Canada Inc.
Byung Jae Park,
President and CEO
75 Frontenac Dr.
Markham, ON L3R 6H2

I

"Letters of thanks, letters from banks,
Letters of joy from girl and boy,
Receipted bills and invitations
To inspect new stock or visit relations,
And applications for situations,
And timid lovers' declarations,
And gossip, gossip from all the nations."

W.H. Auden, Night Mail

Iacobucci, Frank Justice, Supreme Court of Canada	Supreme Court Bldg. Wellington St. Ottawa, ON K1A 0J1
IBM Canada Ltd. William A. Etherington, President and CEO	3500 Steeles Ave. E. Markham, ON L3R 2Z1
Ichino, Yoko *ballerina*	c/o The National Ballet of Canada 157 King St. E. Toronto, ON M5C 1G9
Ignatieff, Michael *writer/historian*	37 Baalbec Rd. London N5 1QN, England
IMAGINE Canadian Centre for Philanthropy Douglas G. Franklin, President and CEO	1329 Bay St., 2nd fl. Toronto, ON M5R 2C4
Imasco Ltd. Purdy Crawford, Chairman and CEO	600 de Maisonneuve ouest Montreal, PQ H3A 3K7

IMAX Corporation
Bradley Wechsler, CEO
giant screen film company
45 Charles St. E.
Toronto, ON M4Y 1S2

Imlach, Punch
former NHL coach
c/o Hockey Hall of Fame
and Museum
BCE Place
30 Yonge St.
Toronto, ON M5E 1X8

Imperial Oil Ltd.
Robert Byron Peterson,
Chairman and CEO
111 St. Clair Ave. W.
Toronto, ON M4W 1K3

Imperial Order Daughters of the Empire (IODE),
National Chapter of Canada
Jean Throop, President
254–40 Orchard View Blvd.
Toronto, ON M4R 1B9

Inco Limited
Michael D. Sopko,
Chairman and CEO
international nickel mining company
Royal Trust Tower
Toronto-Dominion Centre
Toronto, ON M5K 1N4

Infidels
rock band
273 Richmond St. W.
Toronto, ON M5V 1X1

Inner Peace Movement of Canada
promotes self-help techniques
1106 100 Bronson Ave.
Ottawa, ON K1R 6G8

Insight Canada Research
Michael Marzolini, President
polling firm
101 Yorkville Ave.
Ste. 301
Toronto, ON M5R 1C1

Insurance Bureau of Canada
George D. Anderson,
President and CEO
181 University Ave.
13th fl.
Toronto, ON M5H 3M7

International Association of Turtles
Gordon Gray, Director
promotes fellowship and frivolity among all people
P.O. Box 210
Bassano, AB T0J 0B0

International Centre for Human Rights and Democratic Development
Ed Broadbent, President
63 rue de Brésoles
Montreal, PQ H2Y 1V7

International Civil Aviation Organization (ICAO)
Phillipe Rochat,
Secretary General
1000 Sherbrooke St. W.
Montreal, PQ H3A 3G4

International Development Research Centre (IDRC)
Keith Bezanson, President
P.O. Box 8500
Ottawa, ON K1G 3H9

International Federation of Bodybuilders
Ben Weider, President
2875 Bates Rd.
Montreal, PQ H3S 1B7

International Institute for Sustainable Development
Arthur Hanson, President
161 Portage Ave. E.
6th fl.
Winnipeg, MB R3B 0Y4

International Joint Commission
Claude Lanthier, Chairman
oversees Canada-U.S. transborder air and water issues
100 Metcalfe St.
Ottawa, ON K1P 5M1

International Museum of Humour
2111 boul. St-Laurent
Montreal, PQ H2Y 3T9

International Save the Pun Foundation
John S. Crosbie, Chairman
"Literacy Through Wordplay"
P.O. Box 5040, Stn. A
Toronto, ON M5W 1N4

Inuit Broadcasting Corporation (IBC)
Debbie Brisebois,
Executive Director
#703, 251 Laurier Ave. W.
Ottawa, ON K1P 5J6

Ipeelee, Osuitok
Inuit sculptor
Cape Dorset, NT X0A 0C0

Ireland Fund of Canada
Catherine Graham, Chairman
51 Front St. E.
Toronto, ON M5E 1B3

Irvin, Dick
sports broadcaster
c/o CBC–Montreal
P.O. Box 6000
Montreal, PQ H3C 3A8

Irving, Arthur, James, & John
owners of the Irving dynasty
300 Union St., Box 5777
Saint John, NB E2L 4M3

Irwin, Ron
federal Liberal Cabinet Minister
from Ontario
Room 405–WB
House of Commons
Ottawa, ON K1A 0A6

Irwin Toy Ltd.
Samuel Macdonald Irwin,
President and Director
43 Hanna Ave.
Toronto, ON M6K 1X6

Islamic Society of
North America (ISNA)
Dr. Syed Imtiaz Ahmad,
President
P.O. Box 160, Stn. P
Toronto, ON M5S 2S7

Island Telephone Co. Ltd.
Frederick Morash
President and CEO
69 Belvedere Ave.
P.O. Box 820
Charlottetown, PE C1A 7M1

Issajenko, Angela
Canada's fastest woman sprinter
c/o Canada's Sports Hall of Fame
Exhibition Place
Toronto, ON M6K 3C3

Itani, Frances
author
1400 Plumber Ave.
Ottawa, ON K1K 4A9

Ito, Robert
actor
c/o 205 S. Beverly Dr.
Ste. 210
Beverly Hills, CA 90212
U.S.A.

J

"Take away the sword; states can be saved without it; bring the pen."

Edward G. Bulwer-Lytton

Jackman, Hal
Lieutenant-Governor of Ontario

Office of the Lieutenant-Governor
Queen's Park
Toronto, ON M7A 1A1

Jackman, Nancy
philanthropist/feminist

184 Roxborough Dr.
Toronto, ON M4W 1X8

Jackson, Donald
first Canadian to win a world men's figure skating title (1962)

c/o Canada's Sports Hall of Fame
Exhibition Place
Toronto, ON M6K 3C3

Jackson, Russ
former CFL great/ school principal

c/o John Fraser Secondary School
2665 Erin Centre Blvd.
Mississauga, ON L5M 5H6

Jackson, Tom
actor/singer

c/o CBC–North of 60
P.O. Box 500, Stn. A
Toronto, ON M5W 1E6

Jacobs, Jane
author/urban affairs expert

69 Albany Ave.
Toronto, ON M5R 3C2

Jacobs, Joseph
sculptor

c/o Whetung Ojibwa Craft
and Nature Art Gallery
Curve Lake
Buckhorn, ON K0L 1J0

Jaguar Canada Inc.
E. John Mackie, President

8 Indell Lane
Bramalea, ON L6T 4H3

James, Colin
rock singer

c/o Homestead Productions
1616 W. 3rd Ave.
Vancouver, BC V6J 1K2

James, John
rock singer

c/o The Agency
41 Britain St., Ste. 200
Toronto, ON M5A 1R7

Jane Austen Society of North America
Eileen Sutherland, President

4169 Lions Ave.
North Vancouver, BC V7R 3S2

Janvier, Alex
Native artist

P.O. Box 8130
Cold Lake, AB T0A 0V0

Janz, Paul
rock singer/songwriter

c/o 201–1505 W. 2nd Ave.
Vancouver, BC V6H 3Y4

Jeff Healey Band
rock band

c/o The Agency
41 Britain St., Ste. 200
Toronto, ON M5R 2V6

Jehovah's Witnesses
Kenneth Little,
Executive Director

P.O. Box 4100
Georgetown, ON L76 4Y4

Jelinek, Otto
former federal Conservative Cabinet Minister from Ontario
figure skating champion

182 Brookfield Cres.
Oakville, ON L6K 1A9

Jenkins, Ferguson "Fergie"
Baseball Hall of Fame pitcher

12701 N. Pennsylvania
Oklahoma City, OK 73120
U.S.A.

Jennings, Peter
ABC news anchor

c/o ABC Press Relations
77 W. 66th St.
New York, NY 10023, U.S.A.

Jerome, James
Justice, Court of Canada/
former speaker of the House of Commons

Supreme Court Bldg.
Wellington St.
Ottawa, ON K1A 0H9

Jessiman, Duncan
Conservative Senator from Manitoba

Room 623-VB
The Senate
Ottawa, ON K1A 0A4

Jewison, Norman *film producer/director*	Yorktown Productions Ltd. 18 Gloucester St., 5th fl. Toronto, ON M4Y 1L5
Jockey Club of Canada Nigel P.H. Wallace, Executive Director	P.O. Box 156 Rexdale, ON M9W 5L2
Jodrey, John J. *industrialist*	Prince St. Hantsport, NS B0P 1P0
Joe, Mendelson *painter/singer*	c/o Robert Ennis Penthouse 4 Deer Park Cres. Toronto, ON M4V 2C3
Joe, Rita *Native poet/writer/elder*	R.R. #2 East Bay, NS B0A 1H0
John Deere Ltd. Greg Clark, President	P.O. Box 1000 Grimsby, ON L3M 4H5
John Howard Society of Canada James M. MacLatchie, National Director	55 Parkdale Ave. Ottawa, ON K1Y 1E5
Johnson, Albert Wesley "Al" former CBC President	1042 Castle Hill Cres. Ottawa, ON K2C 2A8
Johnson, Ben *runner*	c/o Ed Futerman 2 St. Clair Ave. E. Ste. 1500 Toronto, ON M4T 2R1
Johnson, Daniel Premier of Quebec	Hôtel du Parlement Québec, PQ G1A 1A4
Johnson, C. David *actor*	c/o Gary Goddard & Assoc. 501 Yonge St., Ste. 208 Toronto, ON M4Y 1Y4
Johnson, Janis Conservative Senator from Manitoba	Room 365-E The Senate Ottawa, ON K1A 0A4
Johnson, Pierre-Marc former Premier of Quebec	770 Sherbrooke ouest Ste. 2300 Montreal, Que. H3A 1G1

Johnston, Rita
former Premier of B.C./*first Canadian woman premier*

6595 King George Hwy.
Surrey, BC V3W 4Z4

Jonas, George
writer/author

c/o MGA Agency
10 St. Mary St., Ste. 510
Toronto, ON M4Y 1P9

Jones, Oliver
jazz pianist

c/o SOCAN
1240 Bay St.
Toronto, ON M5Y 2A7

Jordan, Sass
singer

c/o The Agency
41 Britain St., Ste. 200
Toronto, ON M5A 1R7

Journal de Montréal
Yvon Lamarre, Publisher

4545 rue Frontenac
Montreal, PQ H2H 2R7

Journey's End Corp.
Maurice H. Rollins, Chairman and CEO

100, 199 Front St.
Belleville, ON K8N 5H5

Juneau, Pierre
former CBC President

165 ch. Ste-Catherine
app. #1003
Outremont, PQ H2V 2A7

K

"Some men rob you with a six gun,
Some with a fountain pen."

Woody Guthrie, "Pretty Boy Floyd"

Kain, Karen
Principal Dancer

c/o The National Ballet of Canada
157 King St. E.
Toronto, ON M5C 1G9

Kaiser Resources Ltd.
Edgar F. Kaiser, Jr.,
Chairman, President, and CEO

1500 West Georgia St.
20th fl.
Vancouver, BC V6G 2Z8

Kaldor, Connie
folk singer/songwriter

c/o Jim Flemming & Assoc.
733 N. Main St.
Ann Arbor, MI 48104
U.S.A.

Kanata Hotels Ltd.
Willem Jacob Bijl, President
and CEO

489 Queen St. E.
Ste. 101
Toronto, ON M5A 1V1

Kane, Tommy
NFL pro

c/o Seattle Seahawks
11220 NE 53rd St.
Kirkland, WA 98033-7595
U.S.A.

**Karen Jamieson Dance
Company**

185 11th Ave. E.
Vancouver, BC V5T 2C1

Karsh, Yousuf
photographer

Karsh Photographic Studio
Ste. 660, Château Laurier
1 Rideau St.
Ottawa, ON K1N 8S7

Kashtan, William former Chairperson, Communist Party of Canada	24 Cecil St. Toronto, ON M5T 1N2
Kashtin ("Tornado") *Montagnais rock duo*	Maliotenam, PQ G4R 4K2
Kattan, Naim *writer/Canada Council executive*	3463 rue Ste-Famille app. 2114 Montreal, PQ H2X 2K7
Kay, Guy Gavriel *author*	c/o MGA Agency 10 St. Mary St., Ste. 510 Toronto, ON M4Y 1P9
Keegstra, Jim *convicted "Jewish conspiracy" promoter*	Eckville, AB T0M 0X0
Kelleher, James Conservative Senator/former federal Cabinet Minister from Ontario	Room 203-EB The Senate Ottawa, ON K1A 0A4
Keith, Vicki *marathon swimmer*	c/o Swim Ontario 1220 Sheppard Ave. E. Willowdale, ON M2K 2X1
Kelly, William M. Conservative Senator from Ontario	Room 289-S The Senate Ottawa, ON K1A 0A4
Kelly, William P. (Bill) *labour negotiator/former federal public servant*	60 Sullivan Ave. Nepean, ON K2G 1V2
Kennedy, Betty "Front Page Challenge" *panellist/journalist*	68 Old Mill Rd. Toronto, ON M8X 1G8
Kenny, Colin Liberal Senator from Ontario	Room 906G-VB The Senate Ottawa, ON K1A 0A4
Kenojuak *Inuit artist*	c/o West Baffin Eskimo Co-operative Cape Dorset, NWT X0A 0C0

Kent, Arthur
host, CBC's "Man Alive"/the "scud-stud"
c/o CBC–Man Alive
P.O. Box 500, Stn. A
Toronto, ON M5W 1E6

Kent, Peter
Global news anchor
c/o Global TV
81 Barber Greene Rd.
Don Mills, ON M3C 2A2

Kent, Tom
writer/former federal civil servant
Box 29, R.R. #1
Inverary, ON K0H 1X0

Keon, Dr. Wilbert J.
heart surgeon
Conservative Senator from Ontario
11 Barlow Cres.
Dunrobin, ON K0A 1T0

Key Porter Books
Anna Porter,
Publisher and President
70 The Esplanade
Toronto, ON M5E 1R2

Kidder, Margot
actress
8428 Melrose Pl., Ste. C
West Hollywood, CA 90069
U.S.A.

Kids Help Phone/Jeunesse J'Ecoute (1-800-668-6868)
Shelagh Tippet-Fagyas,
Executive Director
#100, 2 Bloor St. W.
P.O. Box 513
Toronto, ON M4W 3E2

Kids in the Hall
TV comedy show
c/o CBC–Kids in the Hall
P.O. Box 500, Stn. A
Toronto, ON M5W 1E6

Kierans, Eric
former federal Liberal Cabinet Minister from Nova Scotia
political commentator
1000 Winwick Rd.
Halifax, NS B3H 4L5

King, Allan
film producer/director
c/o Ralph Zimmerman
Great North Artists Mgmt.
350 Dupont St.
Toronto, ON M5R 1V9

Kinsella, Noel A.
Conservative Senator from New Brunswick
Room 900-VB
The Senate
Ottawa, ON K1A 0A4

Kinsella, W.P.
author
P.O. Box 2162
Blaine, WA 98230
U.S.A.

Kinsmen Clubs
Hal Rogers, Founder
7 Overbrook Cres.
Don Mills, ON M3A 1W1

Kirby, Bruce
designer of the world's most popular sailboat, the Laser, and the America's Cup "Challenger"
213 Rowayton Ave.
Rowayton, CT 06853
U.S.A.

Kirby, Michael J.
Liberal Senator from Nova Scotia
political commentator
Room 204-VB
The Senate
Ottawa, ON K1A 0A4

Kirk, Harvey
host, "Sketches of Our Town"
former TV news anchor
c/o CTV–Sketches of Our Town
250 Yonge St., 18th fl.
Toronto, ON M5B 2L7

Kirkland, Douglas
glamour photographer
9060 Wonderland Park Ave.
Los Angeles, CA 90046
U.S.A.

Kline, Ralph
Premier of Alberta
The Premier's Office
Legislative Building
Edmonton, AB T5K 2B6

Kmart Canada Ltd.
Donald A. Beaumont, President and CEO
8925 Torbram Rd.
Brampton, ON L6T 4G1

Knowles, Stanley H.
former federal NDP MP/ Lifetime Officer of the House of Commons
17 Apache Cres.
Ottawa, ON K2E 6H8

Koffman, Moe
musician/composer
c/o Swinging Shepherd Enterprises
60 Duncannon Dr.
Toronto, ON M5P 2M2

Kogawa, Joy
author
447 Montrose Ave.
Toronto, ON M6G 3H2

Kolber, Leo
Liberal Senator from B.C.
Room 161-S
The Senate
Ottawa, ON K1A 0A4

Korman, Gordon
author
20 Dersingham Cres.
Thornhill, ON L3T 4E7

Kotcheff, Ted
film director/producer

c/o Todd Smith, CAA
1888 Century Park E.
Los Angeles, CA 90067-1702
U.S.A.

Kraft General Foods Canada Inc.
Douglas A. Smith, President

P.O. Box 1200
Don Mills, ON M3C 3J5

Kreskin, "The Amazing"
mentalist/hypnotist

P.O. Box 1383
Caldwell, NJ 07007-1383
U.S.A.

Kricfalusi, John
Creator, "The Ren and Stimpy Show"

Metrocel Animatio Studios
c/o MTV Network
1515 Broadway
New York, NY 10036, U.S.A.

Kroeger, Arthur
Chancellor, Carleton University
former senior federal public servant

245 Springfield Rd.
Ottawa, ON K1M 0L1

K-Tel International Ltd.

21 Murray Park Rd.
Winnipeg, MB R3J 3S2

Kuerti, Anton
pianist

20 Linden St.
Toronto, ON M4Y 1V6

Kuptana, Rosemarie
President, Inuit Tapirisat of Canada

170 Laurier Ave. W.
Ste. 510
Ottawa, ON K1P 5V5

Kuzyk, Mimi
actress

c/o A.C.I. Talent Inc.
205 Ontario St.
Rear Studio
Toronto, ON M5A 2V6

Kwong, Norm
Director, Calgary Flames
former Canadian football great

P.O. Box 1540, Stn. M
Calgary, AB T2P 3B9

L

"Let me hear from thee by letters."

Shakespeare,
"The Two Gentlemen of Verona"

Labatt Breweries of Canada
Sidney M. Oland,
President and CEO

Labatt House
181 Bay St., Ste. 200
Toronto, ON M5J 2T3

L'actualité
Jean Paré, Publisher
French-language current affairs magazine

1001 de Maisonneuve ouest
Montreal, PQ H3A 3E3

Lafleur, Guy
former hockey player

7400 rue Anne Barbel
Quebec, PQ G2K 2C4

La Forest, Gerard
Justice, Supreme Court of Canada

Supreme Court of Canada
Wellington St.
Ottawa, ON K1A 0J1

Laidlaw Inc.
Donald Jackson,
President and CEO

P.O. Box 5028
Burlington, ON L7R 3Y8

Lakehead University
R.G. Rosehart, President

P.O. Box P, Oliver Rd.
Thunder Bay, ON P7B 5E1

La La La Human Steps
Edouard Lock, Choreographer
modern dance group

601–3575 boul. St-Laurent
Montreal, PQ H2X 2T7

La Leche League Canada
organization that promotes breastfeeding

493 Main St.
Winchester, ON K0C 2K0

L'Allier, Jean-Paul
Mayor of Quebec City

C.P. 700
Quebec, PQ G1R 4S9

Lalonde, Bobby *country singer*	P.O. Box 21 Fournier, ON K0B 1G0
Lalonde, Marc former federal Liberal Cabinet Minister from Quebec	c/o Stikeman, Elliott 1155 boul. René-Lévesque ouest, Ste. 3900 Montreal, PQ H3B 3V2
Lam, David C. Lieutenant-Governor of B.C.	Government House 1401 Rockland Ave. Victoria, BC V8S 1V9
Lamarre, Bernard Chairman, Canadian Cultural Property Export Review Board/ former Chairman, Lavalin Inc.	300 Slater St., Ste. 500 Ottawa, ON K1A 0C8
Lambert, Phyllis Director, Canadian Centre for Architecture/*architect*	1920 Baile St. Montreal, PQ H3H 2S6
Lamer, Antonio Chief Justice, Supreme Court of Canada	Supreme Court of Canada Wellington St. Ottawa, ON K1A 0J1
Lamontagne, J. Gilles former Lieutenant-Governor of Quebec/federal Liberal Cabinet Minister	8 Jardins Merici, app. 1405 Quebec, PQ G1S 4N9
Lamoureux, Lucien *diplomat*/former federal Liberal Cabinet Minister from Ontario	96A av. Franklin Roosevelt 1050 Brussels, Belgium
Landsberg, Michele *journalist/writer*	c/o *The Toronto Star* One Yonge St. Toronto, ON M5E 1E6
Lang, Daniel A. Independent Senator from Ontario	Room 389-S The Senate Ottawa, ON K1A 0A4
lang, k.d. *Grammy and Juno award-winning* *singer/songwriter/actress*	c/o The Agency 41 Britain St., Ste. 200 Toronto, ON M5A 1R7

Lang, Otto
former federal Liberal Cabinet Minister from Saskatchewan/ President and CEO, CentraGas Manitoba

CentraGas Manitoba
444 St. Mary Ave.
Winnipeg, MB R3C 3T7

Lanois, Daniel
singer/songwriter/producer

9830 Wilshire Blvd.
Beverly Hills, CA 90212
U.S.A.

Lansdowne, James Fenwick
artist

941 Victoria Ave.
Victoria, BC V8S 4N6

Lantos, Robert
President,
Alliance Entertainment Corp.
film director/producer

920 Yonge St., Ste. 400
Toronto, ON M4W 3C7

LaPalme, Robert
Founder and Director, International Centre of Universal Humour
caricaturist

1081 St-Urbain, S/605
Montreal, PQ H2Z 1K8

La Pierre, Laurier
journalist/author

c/o CJOH TV
1500 Merivale Rd.
Ottawa, ON K2E 6Z5

La Presse
Roger D. Landry, Publisher

7 rue St-Jacques
Montreal, PQ H2Y 1K9

LaSalle, Roch
former federal Conservative Cabinet Minister from Quebec

400 1ere av.
Crabtree, PQ J0K 1B0

Latraverse, Louise
actress/comedian

3625 av. Laval
Montreal, PQ H2X 3E1

Laumann, Silken
Olympic rowing champion

c/o Rowing Canada
1600 James Naismith Dr.
Ste. 716
Gloucester, ON K1B 5N4

Laura Henderson's Clip & Save Exchange
coupon exchange service

36 Strathmanor Dr.
Bowmanville, ON L1C 4L3

Laura Secord Inc.
Bob Leonidas, General Manager

1500 Birchmount Rd.
Scarborough, ON M1P 2G5

The Laurentian Group Corp.
Jacques Drouin, Chairman

1100 boul. René-Lévesque
ouest, 25th fl.
Montreal, PQ H3B 4N4

Laurentian University
Ross H. Paul, President

Ramsey Lake Rd.
Sudbury, ON P3E 2C6

Laval University
Michel Gervais, Rector

Cite universitaire
Quebec, PQ G1K 7P4

Lavoie, Serge
Principal Dancer

c/o The National Ballet of Canada
157 King St. E.
Toronto, ON M5C 1G9

Lavoie, Daniel
rock singer

451 Ste-Sulpice, 4e
Montreal, PQ H2S 2E2

Lavoie-Roux, Thérèse
Conservative Senator from B.C.

Room 577-S
The Senate
Ottawa, ON K1A 0A4

Lawson, Edward M.
Independent Senator from B.C.

Room 556-N
The Senate
Ottawa, ON K1A 0A4

Lawson, Guy
host, TVO's "Imprint"

c/o TVOntario
2180 Yonge St.
Toronto, ON M4S 2C1

Laxer, James
author/political scientist

Dept. of Political Science
York University
4700 Keele St.
North York, ON M3J 1P3

Layton, Irving
poet

6879 Monkland Ave.
Montreal, PQ H4B 1J5

Leader-Post
Edward Schultz, Publisher

P.O. Box 2020
Regina, SK S4P 3G4

League of Canadian Poets
Angela Ribeiro,
Executive Director

24 Ryerson Ave.
Toronto, ON M5T 2P3

Leblanc, Roméo
Speaker of the Senate/former federal Liberal Cabinet Minister from New Brunswick

Room 280-F
The Senate
Ottawa, ON K1A 0A4

LeBreton, Marjory
Conservative Senator from Ontario

Room 279-EB
The Senate
Ottawa, ON K1A 0A4

Le Château
Herschel Segal, President
clothing retail chain

5695 Ferrier St.
Mount Royal, PQ H4P 1N1

Le Devoir
Lise Bissonnette, Publisher

211 St-Sacrement
Montreal, PQ H2Y 1X1

Lee, Dennis
children's author/songwriter

c/o MGA Agency
10 St. Mary St., Ste. 510
Toronto, ON M4Y 1P9

Lee, James M.
former Premier, P.E.I.

Stanhope, R.R. #1
Little York, PE C1A 1P0

Lee-Gartner, Kerrin
Olympic gold medal skier

c/o Alpine Canada
1600 James Naismith Dr.
Ste. 408
Gloucester, ON K1B 5N4

Leger, Viola
"La Sagouine" actress

C.P. 39
Moncton, NB E1C 8R9

Leloup, Jean
rock singer

3973 rue Henri-Julien
Montreal, PQ H2W 2K1

Lemaire, Jacques
General Manager,
New Jersey Devils
former hockey player

c/o New Jersey Devils
Brendan Byrne Arena
Box 504
East Rutherford, NJ 07073
U.S.A.

Lemelin, Stéphane
pianist

c/o Marie Rakos Concert Management
14 Palsen St.
Nepean, ON K2G 2V8

Lemieux, Mario
hockey player

c/o Pittsburgh Penguins
Civic Arena
Pittsburgh, PA 15219 U.S.A.

Lepin, Jacques
Radio-Canada journalist

c/o Radio-Canada
C.P. 6000
succ. Centre Ville
Montreal, PQ H3C 3A8

Lepine, Jean-Francois
Radio-Canada TV
journalist/host, "Le Point"

c/o Radio-Canada–Le Point
C.P. 6000
succ. Centre Ville
Montreal, PQ H3C 3A8

Lesiège, Alexandre
Canadian chess champion

#3, 2145 rue Papineau
Longueuil, PQ J4K 3P6

Leslie Spit Treeo
rock group

14 Sumach St.
Toronto, ON M5A 3J4

Le Soleil
Gilbert Lacasse, Publisher

390 St-Vallier est
Quebec, PQ G1K 7J6

Levine, Norman
author

c/o Penguin Books Canada
10 Alcorn Ave., Ste. 300
Toronto, ON M4V 3B2

Levi Strauss & Co. (Canada) Inc.
John V. DeShano, President

80 Allstate Pkwy.
Markham, ON L3R 8X6

Levy, Eugene
actor/comedian

c/o The Talent Group
387 Bloor St. E., 3rd fl.
Toronto, ON M4W 1H7

Lewis, Derek
Liberal Senator from
Newfoundland

Room 459-S
The Senate
Ottawa, ON K1A 0A4

Lewis, Stephen
Ontario government adviser/
former Ontario NDP Leader and
Ambassador to the UN

6 Montclair Ave.
Toronto, ON M4V 1W1

L'Heureux-Dubé, Claire
Justice, Supreme Court
of Canada

Supreme Court of Canada
Wellington St.
Ottawa, ON K1A 0J1

Liberal Party of Canada
Donald J. Johnston, President

200 Laurier Ave. West
Ottawa, ON K1P 6M7

Libertarian Party of Canada
George Dance, Leader

301–1 St. John's Rd.
Toronto, ON M6P 4C7

Library of Parliament
Erik Spicer, Parliamentary
Librarian

Parliament Buildings
Wellington St.
Ottawa, ON K1A 0A9

Lightfoot, Gordon
singer/songwriter

c/o Early Morning Productions
1365 Yonge St., Ste. 207
Toronto, ON M4T 2P7

Lindros, Eric
hockey player

c/o Philadelphia Flyers
Pattison Place
Philadelphia, PA 19148
U.S.A.

Lions Club International
Roger Lacroix, Secretary

#227, 6 Lansing Sq.
Willowdale, ON M2J 1T5

Lipsey, Richard G.
economist

Simon Fraser University
Economics Dept.
515 West Hastings St.
Vancouver, BC V6B 5K3

Little, Rich
impressionist/comedian

10100 Santa Monica Blvd.
#1600
Los Angeles, CA 90067 U.S.A.

Livesay, Dorothy
poet/journalist/social worker

c/o Peter Macnair
P.O. Box 111
Merville, BC V0R 2M0

Loates, Glen
wildlife artist

556 Edward Ave., Ste. 68
Richmond Hill, ON L4C 9Y5

Loblaws Cos. Ltd.
Galen Weston, Chairman
Canada's largest supermarket chain

22 St. Clair Ave. E.
Toronto, ON M4T 2S5

London Free Press
James E. Armitage,
President and Associate Publisher

369 York St., Box 2280
London, ON N6A 4G1

Lorimer, James
Publisher,
James Lorimer & Co. Ltd.

5502 Atlantic St.
Halifax, NS B3H 1G4

Lotto 6/49
Elizabeth Knebli,
General Manager

c/o Interprovincial Lottery Corporation
1835 Yonge St., Ste. 600
Toronto, ON M4S 1X8

Lougheed, Peter
former Premier of Alberta

4500 Bankers Hall East
855 2nd St. S.W.
Calgary, AB T2P 4K7

Loverboy
rock group

c/o Lou Blair Mgmt. Inc.
68 Water St., Ste. 407
Vancouver, BC V6B 1A4

Luba
rock singer/songwriter

c/o The Agency
41 Britain St., Ste. 200
Toronto, ON M5A 1R7

Lucier, Paul
Liberal Senator from the Yukon

Room 163–S
The Senate
Ottawa, ON K1A 0A4

Lucy Maud Montgomery Birthplace

c/o Buddie MacEwen
P.O. Box 737
Kensington, PE C0B 1M0

Lukacs, Attila Richard
artist

c/o Diane Farris Gallery
1565 7th St. West
Vancouver, BC V6J 1S1

Lundstrom, Linda
fashion designer

33 Mallard Rd.
North York, ON M3B 1S2

Lynch, Charles
journalist/author

36 rue Cartier
Gatineau, PQ J8T 5L1

Lynch, Paul M.
horror film director

c/o Questcan Inc.
1720 Pacific Ave., #303
Los Angeles, CA 90291
U.S.A.

Lynch-Staunton, John
Conservative Senator from Quebec

Room 279-S
The Senate
Ottawa, ON K1A 0A4

Lyon, Sterling
Justice, Manitoba Court of Appeal/former Premier of Manitoba

705 South Dr.
Winnipeg, MB R3T 0C2

M

"She'll wish there was more,
and that's the great art o' letter-writin'."

Charles Dickens,
Pickwick Papers

Macdonald, Donald former federal Liberal Cabinet Minister from Ontario and High Commissioner to the U.K.	27 Marlborough Ave. Toronto, ON M5R 1X5
MacDonald, Finlay Conservative Senator from Nova Scotia/*broadcaster*	Room 229-EB The Senate Ottawa, ON K1A 0A4
Macdonald, Flora former federal Conservative Cabinet Minister from Ontario/ Chairman, International Development Research Centre	350 Queen Elizabeth Dr. Ste. 502 Ottawa, ON K1S 3N1
MacDonald, John M. Conservative Senator from Nova Scotia	Room 571-S The Senate Ottawa, ON K1A 0A4
MacEachen, Allan J. Liberal Senator from Nova Scotia/former federal Cabinet Minister	Room 381-S The Senate Ottawa, ON K1A 0A4
MacIver, Daniel *writer/director*	6 Alpha Ave. Toronto, ON M4X 1J3
Mackasey, Bryce former federal Liberal Cabinet Minister from Quebec	1125 Moffat Ave. Verdun, PQ H4H 1Z1

Mackenzie, Maj. Gen. Louis
former Commander of UN
Forces in Yugoslavia/*television commentator*

c/o Baton Broadcasting
9 Channel Nine Court
Scarborough, ON M1S 4B5

Mackenzie, Michael
Superintendent of Financial
Institutions

255 Albert St., 13th fl.
Ottawa, ON K1A 0H2

MacLaren, Roy
federal Liberal Cabinet Minister
from Ontario

Room 363–WB
House of Commons
Ottawa, ON K1A 0A6

MacLean, J. Angus
former Premier of P.E.I.

R.R. #3
Belle River, PE C0A 1B0

MacLean, Steve
astronaut

Space Station Program
Canadian Space Agency
P.O. Box 7277
Vanier, ON K1L 8E3

MacLean, Vincent (Vince)
former Nova Scotia Liberal Leader

62 Milton St.
Sydney, NS B1P 4L8

Maclean Hunter Ltd.
Ronald W. Osborne,
President and CEO

Maclean Hunter Bldg.
777 Bay St.
Toronto, ON M5W 1A7

***Maclean's* magazine**
Brian Segal, Publisher

777 Bay St.
Toronto, ON M5W 1A7

Maclear, Michael P.
TV broadcaster/author

85 Roxborough St. W.
Toronto, ON M5R 1T9

MacMillan Bloedel Ltd.
Robert Findlay, CEO

1075 West Georgia St.
Vancouver, BC V6E 3R9

Macmillan Canada
Robert J. Dees, President
book publishing firm

29 Birch Ave.
Toronto, ON M4V 1E2

MacNeil, Rita
Cape Breton singer

4881 Yonge St., Ste. 412
Toronto, ON M2N 5X3

MacNeil, Robert
co-anchor, PBS's
"MacNeil/Lehrer Newshour"

c/o WNET/13
356 West 58th St.
New York, NY 10019, U.S.A.

Macquarrie, Heath
Conservative Senator/former MP from P.E.I.
Room 210-EB
The Senate
Ottawa, ON K1A 0A4

Maestro Fresh Wes
rap singer
c/o 1920 Ellesmere Rd.
Ste. 104-376
Scarborough, ON M1H 3G1

Magna International Inc.
Frank Stronach, Chairman
automobile parts manufacturer
36 Apple Creek Blvd.
Markham, ON L3R 4Y4

Magnussen, Karen
world figure skating champion
2852 Thorncliffe Dr.
North Vancouver, BC V7R 2S8

Mahovlich, Frank
former hockey star
c/o Hockey Hall of Fame
BCE Place, 30 Yonge St.
Toronto, ON M5E 1X8

Maillet, Antonine
author/historian/playwright
735 Antonine Maillet Ave.
Montreal, PQ H2V 2Y4

Maitland, Allan
former co-host, CBC's "As It Happens"
c/o CBC Radio
P.O. Box 500, Stn. A
Toronto, ON M5W 1E6

Major, Jack
Justice, Supreme Court of Canada
Supreme Court of Canada
Wellington St.
Ottawa, ON K1A 0J1

Malak (Malak Karsh)
photographer
37 1st. Ave.
Ottawa, ON K1S 2G1

Malarek, Victor
co-host, CBC's "the 5th estate"
c/o CBC–the 5th estate
P.O. Box 500, Stn. A
Toronto, ON M5W 1E6

Malling, Eric
host, CTV's "W5"
c/o CTV–W5
P.O. Box 3000
Agincourt, ON M1S 3C6

Mandel, Eli
author/poet
264 Glenview Ave.
Toronto, ON M4R 1R3

Mandel, Howie
comedian/actor
c/o 9560 Wilshire Blvd., #500
Beverly Hills, CA 90212, U.S.A.

Manguel, Alberto
author/anthologist
45 Geneva Ave.
Toronto, ON M5A 2J9

Manitoba Hydro
Robert B. Brennan,
President and CEO

P.O. Box 815
820 Taylor Ave.
Winnipeg, MB R3C 2P4

Manitoba Telephone System (MTS)
Oz Pedde, President and CEO

P.O. Box 6666
Winnipeg, MB R3C 3V6

Manley, Elizabeth
Olympic figure skater

c/o IMG, 700, 1 St. Clair Ave. E.
Toronto, ON M4T 2V7

Manley, John
federal Liberal Cabinet Minister from Ontario

Room 656–CB
House of Commons
Ottawa, ON K1A 0A6

Mann, Ron
film director

24 Mercer St.
Toronto, ON M5V 1H3

Mann-Borgese, Elisabeth
expert on maritime law

Lester Pearson Institute
Dalhousie University
1321 Edward St.
Halifax, NS B3H 3H5

Manning, Ernest
former Premier of Alberta

P.O. Box 2317
Edmonton, AB T5J 2P4

Manning, Preston
Leader, Reform Party and MP from Alberta

Room 531–S
House of Commons
Ottawa, ON K1A 0A6

Mansbridge, Peter
Chief Correspondent and Co-anchor, CBC's "Prime Time News"

c/o CBC
P.O. Box 14000, Stn. A
Toronto, ON M5W 1A0

Mansouri, Lotfi
opera director

War Memorial Opera House
301 Van Ness Ave.
San Francisco, CA 94102-4509, U.S.A.

Maple Leaf Foods Inc.
David Newton, President
Canada's largest food producer

30 St. Clair Ave. W.
Ste. 1500
Toronto, ON M4V 3A2

Marchand, J.C. de Montigny
Ambassador to Italy/*former senior public servant*

Embassy of Canada
Via G.B. de Rossi 27
00161 Rome, Italy

Marchand, Len
Liberal Senator from B.C.

Room 307-VB
The Senate
Ottawa, ON K1A 0A4

Marchi, Sergio
federal Liberal Cabinet Minister from Ontario

Room 509–CB
House of Commons
Ottawa, ON K1A 0A6

Marcus, Dr. Rudolf
Nobel Prize-winning physicist

c/o California Institute of Technology
1201 E. California Blvd.
Pasadena, CA 91125, U.S.A.

Mariposa Folk Foundation
T. Ann Smiley, President

786 Dundas St. E.
Toronto, ON M4M 1R1

Maritime Telegraph and Telephone Co. Ltd. (MT&T)
Ivan Ernest Hunter Duvar, President and CEO

P.O. Box 880
Halifax, NS B3J 2W3

Marleau, Diane
federal Liberal Cabinet Minister from Ontario

Room 256–CB
House of Commons
Ottawa, ON K1A 0A6

Marshall, Jack
Conservative Senator from Newfoundland

Room 804-VB
The Senate
Ottawa, ON K1A 0A4

Marshall McLuhan Centre on Global Communications
Nelson Thall, President

1 Yonge St.
Toronto, ON K1A 0A6

Martin, Agnes
artist

P.O. Box 35
Galisteo, NM 87540, U.S.A.

Martin, Paul
federal Liberal Cabinet Minister from Quebec

Room 513–S
House of Commons
Ottawa, ON K1A 0A6

Martin, Ted
"Pavlov" cartoonist

29 Bright St.
Toronto, ON M5A 3H5

Mary Kay Cosmetics Ltd.
Arthur R. Patrick, President

5600 Ambler Dr.
Mississauga, ON L4W 2K9

Massé, Marcel
federal Liberal Cabinet Minister from Quebec/former President of CIDA

Room 165–EB
House of Commons
Ottawa, ON K1A 0A6

Masson, Henri L.
artist

1870 Ferncroft Cres.
Ottawa, ON K1H 7B5

Matas, David
human rights lawyer/President,
Canadian Council for Refugees
205 Edmonton St.
Winnipeg, MB R3C 1R4

MATCH-International Centre
Madonna Larbi, Executive Director
Canada's only Third World development agency devoted to women
200 Elgin St., Ste. 1102
Ottawa, ON K1P 1L5

Matheson, Dan
CTV's "Canada AM"
sportscaster and meteorologist
c/o CTV–Canada AM
P.O. Box 3000
Agincourt, ON M1S 3C6

Mawani, Nurjehan
Chairperson, Immigration and Refugee Board
240 Bank St.
Ottawa, ON K1A 0K1

Maxwell, Judith
economist/former Chairman,
Economic Council of Canada
School of Policy Studies
Queen's University
Kingston, ON K7L 3N6

Mazankowski, Don
former federal Conservative
Cabinet Minister from Alberta
P.O. Box 1350
Vegreville, AB T0B 4L0

Mazda Canada Inc.
Toshi Mori, President
821 Brock Rd. S.
Pickering, ON L1W 3L6

McCain, Harrison H.
Chairman, McCain Foods Ltd.
East Florenceville
NB E0J 1K0

McCall, Christina
author/editor
44 Rosedale Rd.
Toronto, ON M4W 2P6

McCarthy, Grace
Leader, B.C. Social Credit Party
Room 101
Parliament Buildings
Victoria, BC V8V 1X4

McCarthy, Sheila
actress
c/o A.C.I. Talent Inc.
205 Ontario St., Rear Studio
Toronto, ON M5A 2V6

McClelland & Stewart
Avie Bennett, Chairman and President
book publishing firm
481 University Ave.
Ste. 900
Toronto, ON M5G 2E9

McCrory, Colleen
environmental activist
Chairperson, The Valhalla Society
c/o *Equinox*
7 Queen Victoria Rd.
Camden East, ON K0K 1J0

McCurdy, Howard
former NDP MP from Ontario
and first black Canadian MP
12213 Papineau Court
Tecumseh, ON N8N 3B5

McDermott, Dennis
former President, Canadian Labour
Congress/*diplomat*
R.R. #1, Buckhorn Sands
Lakefield, ON K0L 2H0

McDonald's Restaurants
of Canada Ltd.
Ronald Cohen, Chairman and CEO
McDonald's Place
Toronto, ON M3C 3L4

McDonough, Alexa
Nova Scotia NDP Leader
1657 Barrington St.
P.O. Box 1617
Halifax, NS B3J 2Y3

McDougall, Barbara
former federal Conservative
Cabinet Minister from Ontario
c/o Board of Directors
SHL Systemhouse Inc.
50 O'Connor St., Ste. 1616
Ottawa, ON K1P 6L2

McFee, Allan
CBC Radio host,
"Eclectic Circus"
c/o CBC–Eclectic Circus
P.O. Box 500, Stn. A
Toronto, ON M5W 1E6

McGibbon, Pauline M.
former Lieutenant Governor of
Ontario and Canada's first
woman Lieutenant-Governor
20 Avoca Ave., Apt. 2004
Toronto, ON M4T 2B8

McGill University
Bernard Shapiro, Principal and
Vice Chancellor
845 Sherbrooke St. W.
Montreal, PQ H3A 2T5

McGrath, Douglas
Goin' Down the Road actor
c/o Oscars and Abrams
59 Berkeley St.
Toronto, ON M5A 2W5

McGrath, James Aloysius
former Lieutenant-Governor of
Newfoundland and federal
Conservative Cabinet Minister
c/o National Transportation
Agency
Ottawa, ON K1A 0N9

McIntyre, Lyndon
co-host, "the 5th estate"
P.O. Box 500, Stn. A
Toronto, ON M5W 1E6

McKay, Rev. Stanley J. Moderator, United Church of Canada	85 St. Clair Ave. E. Toronto, ON M4T 1M8
McKenna, Frank Premier of New Brunswick	P.O. Box 6000 Fredericton, NB E3B 5H1
McKennitt, Loreena *harpist/singer*	P.O. Box 933 Stratford, ON N5A 7M3
McKeown, Robert D. co-host, "the 5th estate"	P.O. Box 500, Stn. A Toronto, ON M5W 1E6
McKoy, Marc *Olympic track & field champion*	c/o Landmark Sport Group 277 Richmond St. W. Toronto, ON M5W 1X1
McLachlan, Sarah *rock musician*	Box 330, 1755 Robson St. Vancouver, BC V6G 3B7
McLachlin, Beverley Justice, Supreme Court of Canada	Supreme Court of Canada Wellington St. Ottawa, ON K1A 0J1
McLauchlan, Murray *folk singer*	41 Britain St., Ste. 200 Toronto, ON M5A 1R7
McLean, George *wildlife artist*	R.R. #1 Bognor, ON N0H 1E0
McLaughlin, Audrey Leader, federal New Democratic Party	Room 649–D House of Commons Ottawa, ON K1A 0A6
McLellan, Anne federal Liberal Cabinet Minister from Alberta	Room 322–WB House of Commons Ottawa, ON K1A 0A6
McLeod, Lyn Liberal Leader, Ontario	Room 223, Legislative Bldg. Toronto, ON M7A 1A4
McMahon, Pat Mayor of Yellowknife	P.O. Box 580 Yellowknife, NT X1A 2N4
McMaster University Geraldine Kenny-Wallace, President	Hamilton, ON L8S 4L8
McMichael Canadian Art Collection Barbara A. Tyler, Director and CEO	Islington Ave. Kleinburg, ON L0J 1C0

McMillan, Charles
Asia expert/former Adviser to the Prime Minister
c/o Asia-Pacific Foundation
666-999 Canada Place
Vancouver, BC V6C 3E1

McQuaig, Linda
author/journalist
551 Gerrard St. E.
Toronto, ON M4M 1X7

McTeer, Maureen
professor/lawyer/Conservative Party activist
c/o School of Public Health
University of California at Berkeley
Berkeley, CA 94720, U.S.A.

MediaWatch
Suzanne Strutt, Executive Director
517 Wellington St. W.
Toronto, ON M5V 1G1

Medina, Ann
journalist/film producer
Chairwoman, Academy of Canadian Cinema and Television
112 Alcina Ave.
Toronto, ON M6G 2E8

Medley, Sue
singer
107 Grenadier Rd.
Toronto, ON M6R 1R1

Meighen, Michael
Conservative Senator from Ontario/*grandson of former Prime Minister*
Room 577–S
The Senate
Ottawa, ON K1A 0A4

Memorial University
Arthur W. May, President
P.O. Box 4200
St. John's, NF A1C 5S7

Men of the Deeps
John C. O'Donnell, Music Director/*coal miners choir*
22 Carroll St.
Glace Bay, NS B1A 3B3

Men Without Hats
rock group
1445 Lambert Closse, #200
Montreal, PQ H3H 1Z5

Mennonite Central Committee Canada
Daniel Zehr, Executive Director
134 Plaza Dr.
Winnipeg, MB R3T 5K9

Mensa Canada Society
Wendy Marsh, Executive Director
the high-I.Q. society
P.O. Box 505, Stn. S
Toronto, ON M5M 4L8

Mercedes-Benz Canada, Inc.
Werner Niefer, Chairman
849 Eglinton Ave. E.
Toronto, ON M4G 2L5

Mercredi, Ovide
Chief, Assembly of First Nations

55 Murray St.
Ottawa, ON K1N 5M3

Mercure, Monique
actress/first woman to head the National Theatre School of Canada

1, 440 Bonsecours
Montreal, PQ H2Y 3C4

Mesley, Wendy
CBC journalist

c/o CBC, P.O. Box 500, Stn. A
Toronto, ON M5W 1E6

Messenjah
reggae band

1971 Spruce Hill Rd.
Pickering, ON L1V 1S6

Messier, Mark
hockey player

c/o New York Rangers
Madison Square Garden
4 Pennsylvania Plaza
New York, NY 10001, U.S.A.

Metcalfe, John
author

P.O. Box 2700, Stn. D
Ottawa, ON K1P 5W7

Metis National Council
Gerald Morin, Leader

50 O'Connor St., Ste. 310
Ottawa, ON K1P 6L2

Michaels, Lorne
producer, "Saturday Night Live"

c/o Broadway Video
1619 Broadway
New York, NY 10019, U.S.A.

Mike and Mike's Excellent Cross-Canada Adventure
Mike Rhodes and Mike Campbell

c/o MuchMusic
299 Queen St. W.
Toronto, ON M5V 2Z5

Mikita, Stan
former hockey player

15 Windsor Dr.
Oak Brook, IL 60521, U.S.A.

Milgaard, David
released after 22 years in prison after Supreme Court of Canada set aside his murder conviction

c/o Hersh E. Wolch
444 St. Mary Ave., 5th fl.
Winnipeg, MB R3C 3T1

Millar, Ian
"Captain Canada"
equestrian champion

Millerbrook Farm
Perth, ON K7H 3C7

Miller, Frank Stuart
former Premier of Ontario

P.O. Box 2198
Bracebridge, ON P1L 1W1

Mills, Frank
pianist/composer

c/o Balmur
4881 Yonge St., Ste. 412
Toronto, ON M2N 5X3

The Miners' Museum	P.O. Box 610 Springhill, NS B0M 1X0
Minglewood, Matt *rock singer*	c/o Supervision 807 Sweetwater Cres. Mississauga, ON L5H 4A7
Mirvish, David *theatrical producer*	266 King St. W., 4th fl. Toronto, ON M5V 1H9
Mirvish, Ed owner, Honest Ed's Ltd.	581 Bloor St. W. Toronto, ON M6G 1K3
Mr. Dressup (Ernest Coombs) *children's TV character*	44 Twyn Rivers Dr. Pickering, ON L1V 1E2
Mistry, Rohinton *author*	c/o McClellan & Stewart 481 University Ave., Ste. 900 Toronto, ON M5G 2E9
Mitchell, Joni (Roberta Joan Anderson) *pop singer/songwriter*	c/o Peter Asher Mgmt. 644 North Doheny Dr. Los Angeles, CA 90069 U.S.A.
Mitchell, Kim *rock singer*	c/o Alert Management 41 Britain St., Ste. 305 Toronto, ON M5A 1R7
Mitchell, W.O. *author*	c/o McClelland & Stewart 481 University Ave., Ste. 900 Toronto, ON M5G 2E9
Mitchibata, Glen *professional tennis player*	c/o Tennis Canada 3111 Steeles Ave. Downsview, ON M3J 3H2
Mitel Corp. Dr. John Millard, President and CEO	350 Legget Dr. Kanata, ON K2H 1Y6
Molgat, Gildas Liberal Senator from Manitoba	Room 252-N The Senate Ottawa, ON K1A 0A4
Molinari, Guido *artist*	3288 St. Catherine St. E. Montreal, PQ H1W 2C6
Molson Breweries of Canada Ltd. C. Carroll, President and CEO	175 Bloor St. E. Toronto, ON M4W 3S4

Molson, Eric H.
Chairman,
The Molson Companies

1555 Notre Dame E.
Montreal, PQ H2L 2R5

Monarchist League of Canada
John Aimers, Chairman

P.O. Box 1057
Oakville, ON L6J 5E9

Money, Maj. Kenneth
astronaut/scientist

c/o DCIEM, DND
P.O. Box 2000
Downsview, ON M3M 3B9

Monk, Lorraine
author

176 Balmoral Ave.
Toronto, ON M4V 1J6

Montréal Canadiens
Serge Savard, General Manager

2313 Ste-Catherine ouest
Montreal, PQ H3H 1N2

Montreal Exchange (ME)
Bruno Riverin, President

The Stock Exchange Tower
800 Victoria Square
Montreal, PQ H4Z 1A9

Montreal Expos
National League baseball team

P.O. Box 500, Stn. M
Montreal, PQ H1V 3N7

Montreal Museum of Decorative Arts
Luc d'Iberville-Moreau, Curator

Chateau Dufresne
C.P. 12000, Succ. A
Montreal, PQ H3C 3P3

Montreal Museum of Fine Arts
Pierre Theberge, Director

P.O. Box 3000, Stn. H
Montreal, PQ H3G 2T9

Montreal Symphony Orchestra
Louise Laplante, Executive Director

85 rue Ste-Catherine ouest
Ste. 900, Montreal, PQ H2X 3P4

Moore, Brian
author

c/o Curtis-Brown Inc.
10 Astor Pl.
New York, NY 10003, U.S.A.

Moore, Mavor
playwright/producer/critic

2826 Arbutus Rd.
Victoria, BC V8N 5X5

Moores, Frank
lobbyist/former Premier of Newfoundland

c/o Government Consultants International
#1300, 50 O'Connor St.
Ottawa, ON K1P 6L2

Moosehead Breweries Ltd.
Derek Oland, President
Canada's largest and oldest independent brewery

656 Windmill Rd.
Dartmouth, NS B3B 1B8

Morden, Reid
Undersecretary of State for External Affairs/former Director, Canadian Security Intelligence Service

Lester B. Pearson Bldg.
125 Sussex Dr.
Ottawa, ON K1A 0G2

Morgentaler, Dr. Henry
abortion advocate

The Morgentaler Clinic
727 Hillsdale Ave. E.
Toronto, ON M4S 1V4

Morin, Jacques-Yvan
law professor/former Parti-Québécois Politician

P.O. Box 6128, Succ. A
Montreal, PQ H3C 3J7

Moriyama, Raymond
architect

32 Davenport Rd.
Toronto, ON M5R 1H3

Morris, Joe
former labour leader

4257 Thornhill Cres.
Victoria, BC V8N 3G6

Morrisseau, Norval
painter

1106 Fir St.
White Rock, BC V4V 4A6

Morrison, Keith
co-host, CTV's "Canada AM"

c/o CTV–Canada AM
P.O. Box 3000
Agincourt, ON M1S 3C6

Morse, Barry
actor/director

506, 71 Charles St. E.
Toronto, ON M4Y 2T3

Morton, Desmond
historian/Principal, Erindale College

362 Queen St. S.
Streetsville, ON L5M 1M2

Moses, Ted
UN Ambassador for the Grand Council of the Crees/Chief, Eastman (Cree) Nation

24 Bayswater Ave.
Ottawa, ON K1Y 2E4

Mothers Against Drunk Drivers/ Canadian Society (MADD)
Sally Gribble, founder/Director

820A, 12th St.
New Westminster BC V3M 4K3

Mount Allison University
Ian Newbould, President

Sackville, NB E0A 3C0

Mount Saint Vincent University
Elizabeth Parr-Johnston, President

Halifax, NS B2M 2J6

Mouvement national des Québécoises et Québécois
Sylvain Simard, President
sovereigntist organization

2207 rue Fullum
Montreal, PQ H2K 3P1

Mouvement Québec Français
Guy Bouthillier, President
promotes the dominance of French in Quebec

82 rue Sherbrooke ouest
Montreal, PQ H2X 1X3

Mowat, Farley
author

c/o Key Porter Books
70 The Esplanade
Toronto, ON M5E 1R2

Moxy Früvous
rock band

c/o The Agency
41 Britain St., Ste. 200
Toronto, ON M5A 1R7

MuchMusic
Moses Znaimer, co-founder/
Executive Producer

299 Queen St. W.
Toronto, ON M5V 2Z5

Muir, Robert
Conservative Senator from Nova Scotia

Room 552-N
The Senate
Ottawa, ON K1A 0A4

Mulligan, Terry David
MuchMusic host/VJ

c/o MuchMusic
299 Queen St. W.
Toronto, ON M5V 2Z5

Mulroney, Brian M.
former Conservative
Prime Minister

c/o Ogilvy Renault
1981 McGill College Ave.
Ste. 1100
Montreal, PQ H3A 3C1

Mulroney, Mila
wife of former Prime Minister
director of Astral Communications

47 Forden Cres.
Montreal, PQ H3Y 2Z1

Munday, Dave
first person to twice ride down Niagara Falls

R.R. #3
Caistor Centre, ON L0R 1E0

Munro, Alice
author

P.O. Box 1133
Clinton, ON N0M 1L0

Munro, John
former federal Liberal Cabinet
Minister from Ontario

1051 Main St. E.
Hamilton, ON L8M 1W5

Munsch, Robert
children's author

15 Sharon Pl.
Guelph, ON N1H 7V2

Murray, Anne
singer

c/o Balmur
412, 4881 Yonge St.
Toronto, ON M2N 5X3

Murray, Lowell
Conservative Senator from Ontario

Room 275–S
The Senate
Ottawa, ON K1A 0A4

Museum for Textiles
Valerie Greenfield, Executive Director
Canada's only textile museum

55 Centre Ave.
Toronto, ON M5G 2H5

Musgrave, Susan
author/columnist

P.O. Box 2421
Sidney, BC V8L 3Y3

Musique Plus
French-language all-music TV channel

209 Ste-Catherine est
Montreal, PQ H2X 1L2

Mussallem, Dr. Helen
Canada's most distinguished nurse

1706, 20 The Driveway
Ottawa, ON K2P 1C8

Myers, Mike
comedian/actor

c/o Saturday Night Live
NBC-TV
30 Rockefeller Plaza
New York, NY 10112
U.S.A.

Myles, Alannah
rock singer

435–3575 Cahuenga Blvd. W.
Los Angeles, CA 90068
U.S.A.

N

"It is curious that the letters we desire to write most should often get delayed.
The casual note, the routine letter, is sent off and yet the letter which we are thinking of most remains unwritten."

Nehru

Narcotics Anonymous Fern Harding, President	P.O. Box 5700, Stn. A Toronto, ON M5W 1N8
Nash, Knowlton *CBC journalist*	c/o CBC Box 500, Stn. A Toronto, ON M5W 1E4
National Action Committee on the Status of Women (NAC) Sunera Thobani, President	57 Mobile Dr. Toronto, ON M4A 1H5
National Anti-Poverty Organization Lynne Toupin, Executive Director	456 Rideau St. Ottawa, ON K1N 5Z4
National Archives of Canada Jean-Pierre Wallot, National Archivist	395 Wellington St. Ottawa, ON K1A 0N3
National Arts Centre (NAC) Yves DesRochers, Director General	P.O. Box 1534, Stn. B Ottawa, ON K1P 5W1

National Arts Centre Orchestra Trevor Pinnock, Principal Conductor	P.O. Box 1534, Stn. B Ottawa, ON K1P 5W1
National Association for English Rights Faye Garner *opposes official bilingualism*	86 King St. E. Brockville, ON K6V 6N5
National Ballet of Canada Reid Anderson, Artistic Director	157 King St. E. Toronto, ON M5C 1G9
National Bank of Canada André Berard, Chairman and CEO	National Bank Tower 600 de la Gauchetière ouest Montreal, PQ H3B 4L2
National Capital Commission (NCC) Marcel Beaudry, Chairman	161 Laurier Ave. W. Ottawa, ON K1P 6J6
National Citizens' Coalition David Somerville, President and CEO *promotes free-market system and a reduced role for government*	100 Adelaide St. W. Ste. 907 Toronto, ON M5H 1S3
National Film Board of Canada (NFB) Joan Pennefather, Film Commissioner	P.O. Box 6100, Stn. A Montreal, PQ H3C 3H5
National Gallery of Canada Shirley L. Thomson, Director	P.O. Box 427, Stn. A Ottawa, ON K1N 9N4
National Hockey League (NHL) Gary Bettman, Commissioner	650 5th Ave. New York, NY 10019 U.S.A.
National Hockey League Players' Association Bob Goodenow, Executive Director	37 Maitland St. Toronto, ON M4Y 1C8
National League Baseball William D. White, President	350 Park Ave., 18th fl. New York, NY 10022 U.S.A.

National Library of Canada Marianne Scott, National Librarian	395 Wellington St. Ottawa, ON K1A 0N4
National Museum of Science and Technology Genevieve Sainte-Marie, Director	P.O. Box 9724, Stn. T Ottawa, ON K1G 5A3
National Party of Canada Bill Loewen, President	250 Portage Ave. Winnipeg, MB R3C 0B5
National Research Council Canada (NRC) Pierre O. Perron, President	Building M58 Montreal Rd. Ottawa, ON K1A 0R6
National Sea Products Ltd. Henry Demone, President	P.O. Box 2130 Halifax, NS B3J 3B7
Native Council of Canada Ron George, President	384 Bank St., #200 Ottawa, ON K2P 1Y4
Natural Law Party of Canada Neil Paterson, Leader *political party whose ultimate goal is heaven on earth*	500 Wilbrod St. Ottawa, ON K1N 6N2
Neiman, Joan Liberal Senator from Ontario	Room 477-S The Senate Ottawa, ON K1A 0A4
Nelligan, Kate *actress*	c/o ICM 321 Westminister Ave. Los Angeles, CA 90020-4652 U.S.A.
Nellis, Zonda *fashion designer*	2203 Granville St. Vancouver, BC V6H 3G1
Nestor, Daniel *tennis star*	c/o Tennis Canada 3111 Steeles Ave. W. Downsview, ON M3J 3H2
Neville, John *stage actor and director*	99 Norman St. Stratford, ON N5A 5R8
Neville, William (Bill) *Lobbyist/Conservative Party strategist*	#700, 99 Bank St. Ottawa, ON K1P 6B9

Newbridge Networks Corp. Terence Matthews, Chairman and CEO	600 March Rd. Kanata, ON K2H 2E6
New Brunswick Power Corp. G.L. (Lin) Titus, President	P.O. Box 2000 Fredericton, NB E3E 4X1
New Brunswick Telephone Co. Ltd. Lino J. Celeste, President and CEO	P.O. Box 1430 Saint John, NB E2L 4K2
New Democratic Party of Canada Nancy Riche, President	310 Somerset St. W. Ottawa, ON K2P 0J9
Newfoundland Light and Power Co. Ltd. Aiden F. Ryan, President and CEO	55 Kenmount Rd. P.O. Box 8910 St. John's, NF A1B 3P6
Newfoundland Telephone Co. Ltd. Anthony Brait, Chairman of the Board	P.O. Box 2110 Fort Williams Bldg. St. John's, NF A1C 5H6
Newman, Don CBC News parliamentary correspondent	c/o CBC News 150 Wellington St., Ste. 800 Ottawa, ON K1P 5A4
Newman, Kevin co-host, CBC's "Midday"	c/o CBC–Midday P.O. Box 500, Stn. A Toronto, ON M5W 1E6
Newman, Peter C. *author/journalist*	c/o *Maclean's* 777 Bay St. Toronto, ON M5W 1A7
CBC Newsworld Michael Harris, President "The All-News Channel"	c/o CBC P.O. Box 500, Stn. A Toronto, ON M5W 1E6
Niagara Institute R. Geoffrey P. Styles, Chairman *economic think tank*	P.O. Box 1041 Niagara-on-the-Lake ON L0S 1J0
Nichol, Dave *Canada's leading grocery marketer*	c/o Loblaws Cos. Ltd. 22 St. Clair Ave. E. Toronto, ON M4T 2S5

Nicholas, Cindy
first woman to complete a two-way crossing of the English Channel (1977)/former Ontario politician
R.R. #5
Claremont, ON L1Y 1A2

Nielsen, Leslie
actor/comedian
15760 Ventura Blvd., #1730
Los Angeles, CA 91436, U.S.A.

Nissan Canada Inc.
Eisuke (Ace) Toyama, President
5290 Orbitor Dr.
Mississauga, ON L4Y 4H6

Nolin, Pierre-Claude
Conservative Senator from Quebec
Room 602-VB
The Senate
Ottawa, ON K1A 0A4

Non-Smokers' Rights Association
Garfield Mahood, Executive Director
#308, 344 Bloor St. W.
Toronto, ON M5S 3A7

Noranda Inc.
Adam H. Zimmerman, Chairman
P.O. Box 7, Ste. 4414
BCE Place, T-D Bank Tower
Toronto-Dominion Centre
Toronto, ON M5K 1A1

Norman Mackenzie Art Gallery
Andrew Oko, Director
3475 Albert St.
Regina, SK S4S 6X6

NORML Canada
(National Organization for the Reform of Marijuana Laws)
Craig MacLachlan, National Director
c/o 228 Westmount Ave.
Toronto, ON M6E 3M8

Norrie, William
Mayor of Winnipeg
510 Main St.
Winnipeg, MB R3B 1B9

North American Chronic Pain Association of Canada
Dianne E. Kent-Cachia, President
6 Handel Ct.
Brampton, ON L6S 1Y4

The Northern Pikes
rock band
c/o 4442 Sawmill Valley Dr.
Mississauga, ON L5L 3N2

Northern Telecom Ltd.
Jean Monty, President and CEO
world's fifth-largest telephone equipment maker
3 Robert Speck Parkway,
Mississauga, ON L4Z 3C8

North-South Institute Maureen O'Neil, President *international affairs think tank*	55 Murray St., Ste. 200 Ottawa, ON K1N 5M3
Nova, Aldo *rock singer*	c/o Baruck-Consolo Mgmt. 15003 Greenleaf St. Sherman Oaks, CA 91403, U.S.A.
Nova Corp. of Alberta J. Ted Newall, President and CEO *pipeline and petrochemical company*	P.O. Box 2535, Stn. M Calgary, AB T2P 2N6
Nova Scotia College of Art and Design (NSCAD) Ian Clark, President	5163 Duke St. Halifax, NS B3J 3J6
Nova Scotia Power Corp. Louis Roland Comeau, President and CEO	P.O. Box 910 Halifax, NS B3J 2W5
Nunavut Tunngavik Inc. Paul Quassa, President *Inuit corporation planning and managing revenues of new Nunavut Territory*	130 Slater St., Ste. 800 Ottawa, ON K1P 6E2
Nuytten, Phil *Newtsuit inventor*	1367 Crown St. North Vancouver, BC V7J 1G4
Northwest Territorial Airways Ltd. (NWT Air) Ben Murphy, General Manager	P.O. Box 9000 Yellowknife, NT X1A 2R3
Nygard, Peter *fashion designer*/Chairman, Nygard International Ltd.	1 Niagara St. Toronto, ON M5V 1C2
Nylons *a cappella musical group*	c/o 273 Richmond St. W. Toronto, ON M5V 1X1

O

"One man was so mad at me that he ended his letter: 'Beware. You will never get out of this world alive.'"

John Steinbeck,
"The Mail I've Seen"

Obomsawin, Alanis *film director/producer*	c/o NFB C.P. 6100 Montréal, PQ H3C 3H5
O Canada Foundation Ross Carlin, President *promotes and perpetuates Canada's national anthem*	P.O. Box 993 Guelph, ON N1H 6N1
Odjig, Daphne *artist/muralist*	P.O. Box 111 Anglemont, BC V0E 1A0
Ogden, Frank *futurist*/"Dr. Tomorrow"	c/o *The Province* 2250 Granville St. Vancouver, BC V6H 3G2
Ogle, Father Robert Joseph *priest*/former Conservative MP	220, 2902 Louise St. Saskatoon, SK S7J 3M2
***Old Fart* magazine** John Brinckman, Publisher *Canada's magazine for curmudgeons*	Box 83509 199 Avenue Rd. Toronto, ON M5R 2J3
Oliver, Donald Conservative Senator from Nova Scotia	Room 473-S The Senate Ottawa, ON K1A 0A4
Olson, Clifford convicted child killer	c/o Special Handling Unit Saskatchewan Penitentiary P.O. Box 160 Prince Albert, SK S6V 5R6

Olson, H.A. (Bud)
Liberal Senator from Alberta
Room 361-E
The Senate
Ottawa, ON K1A 0A4

Ominayak, Bernard
Chief, Lubicon Lake Cree
P.O. Box 6731
Peace River, AB T8S 1S5

Ondaatje, Christopher
investment banker/author
13 Hazelton Ave.
Toronto, ON M5R 2E1

Ondaatje, Michael
Booker Prize-winning author
2275 Bayview Ave.
Toronto, ON M4N 3M6

One Voice: The Canadian Seniors Network
Ivan Hale, National Secretary
#1005–350 Sparks St.
Ottawa, ON K1R 7S8

Onley, Toni
artist
4279 Yuculta Cres.
Vancouver, BC V6N 4A9

Ontario Provincial Police (OPP)
T.B. O'Grady, Commissioner
90 Harbour St.
Toronto, ON M7A 2S1

Ontario Securities Commission (OSC)
Edward Waitzer, Chairman
Canada's leading securities commission
20 Queen St. W., Ste. 1800
Toronto, ON M5H 3R3

Orr, Bobby
former hockey player
647 Summer St.
Boston, MA 02210
U.S.A.

Orser, Brian
Olympic figure skater
35 McKenzie Ave.
Toronto, ON M4W 1K1

Orsini, Marina
actress
c/o Agence Ginette Achim
1439 St-Mathieu
Montreal, PQ H3H 2M4

Osbaldeston, Gordon
former Secretary to the Cabinet
School of Business Administration
University of Western Ontario
London, ON N6A 3K7

Osgoode Hall Law School
Marilyn Pilkington, Dean
4700 Keele St.
North York, ON M3J 1P3

Ostanek, Walter
"The Polka King"
3 Royal York Rd.
St. Catharines, ON L2N 2N7

Ostry, Bernard
former TVO Chairman
P.O. Box 200, Stn. Q
Toronto, ON M4T 2R1

Ostry, Sylvia
international economist
18 Madison Ave.
Toronto, ON M5R 2S1

Ott, Carlos A.
architect
350 Bloor St. E.
Toronto, ON M4W 3S6

Ottawa Citizen
Russel Mills, Publisher
1101 Baxter Rd.
Ottawa, ON K2C 3M4

Ottawa Lynx Baseball Club
Jim Tracey, General Manager
Montreal Expos farm team
1308 Wellington St.
Ottawa, ON K1Y 3B2

Ottawa Rough Riders Football Club
John Ritchie, General Manager
Lansdowne Park,
Ottawa, ON K1S 3W7

Ottawa Senators Hockey Club
Randy Sexton, General Manager
411–301 Moodie Dr.
Nepean, ON K2H 9C4

Ottawa Sun
Hartley Steward, Publisher
380 Hunt Club Rd.
Ottawa, ON K1G 5H7

Ottenheimer, Gerald R.
Conservative Senator from Newfoundland
Room 369-E
The Senate
Ottawa, ON K1A 0A4

Ouellet, André
federal Liberal Cabinet Minister from Quebec
Room 314–WB
House of Commons
Ottawa, ON K1A 1A6

Owen, Philip
Mayor of Vancouver
Office of the Mayor
453 W. 12th Ave.
Vancouver, BC V5Y 1V4

OXFAM-Canada
John W. Foster,
National Secretary
251 Laurier Ave. W.
Ste. 301
Ottawa, ON K1P 5J6

P

"Nine-tenths of the letters in which people speak unreservedly of their inmost thoughts are written after ten at night."

Thomas Hardy

Pace, Kate
downhill ski champion
c/o Kevin Albrecht, IMG
1 St. Clair Ave. E., Ste. 700
Toronto, ON M4T 2V7

Pachter, Charles
artist
2 Grange Place
Toronto, ON MST 2Z5

Pacific Motion Pictures
Matthew O'Connor, President
production company
827 Hamilton Dr.
Vancouver, BC V6B 2R7

Page, P.K.
poet/writer/painter
3260 Exeter Rd.
Victoria, BC V8R 6H6

Pape, Gordon
financial consultant/author
372 Woodsworth Rd.
Willowdale, ON M2L 2T6

Paquet-Sevigny, Thérèse
UN Under-Secretary-General
for Public Information
The United Nations
New York, NY 10017
U.S.A.

Paragon Pictures
Jon Sloan, Chairman and CEO
TV production company
200–1525 W. 8th Ave.
Vancouver, BC V6J 1T5

Paré, Jean
President, Company's Coming
Publishing Ltd.
cookbook publisher
P.O. Box 8037, Stn. F
Edmonton, AB T6H 4N9

Parents Against Drugs
Diane Buhler, Executive Director
70 Maxome Ave.
Willowdale, ON M2M 3K1

Parents Without Partners Inc.
Ralph Patterson
P.O. Box 1218, Stn. B
Oshawa, ON L1J 5Z1

Parizeau, Jacques
Leader, Parti Québécois
Edifice A, Bureau 2.83
Hôtel du Parlement
Quebec, PQ G1A 1A4

Parrot, Jean-Claude
Vice-President,
Canadian Labour Congress
2841 Riverside Dr.
Ottawa, ON K1V 8X7

Parti Québécois (PQ)
Pierre Boileau,
Executive Director
7370 rue St-Hubert
Montreal, PQ H2R 2N3

Patkau, John and Patricia
architects
100–560 Beatty St.
Vancouver, BC V6B 2L3

Patterson, Freeman
photographer
Shampers Bluff
Clifton Royal, NB E0G 1N0

Pattison, Jim
Chairman, President, and CEO,
The Jim Pattison Group
1055 W. Hastings St.
Vancouver, BC V6E 2H2

Pavelic, Myfanwy Spencer
portrait artist
Spencerwood
577 Ardmore Dr., R.R. #2
Sidney, BC V8L 3S1

Pawley, Howard
former Premier of Manitoba
907–75 Riverside Dr. E.
Windsor, ON N9A 2S4

Pearson, Geoffrey
diplomat/son of former Prime Minister
199 Daly Ave.
Ottawa, ON K1N 6G1

Pearson, Peter
film and TV producer/director
417 av. Mount Pleasant
Westmount, PQ H3Y 3G9

Peckford, Brian
former Premier of Newfoundland
570 Newfoundland Dr.
St. John's, NF A1A 5B1

Peers, Most Rev. Michael
Primate, Anglican Church
of Canada
600 Jarvis St.
Toronto, ON M4Y 2J6

Peggy's Cove Lighthouse
Canada's best known lighthouse
Peggy's Cove, NS B0J 2N0

Péladeau, Pierre
President, Quebecor Inc.
612 St. James St.
Montreal, PQ H3C 4M8

Pelletier, Francine
broadcaster/political commentator
c/o *The Gazette*
250 St. Antoine St. W.
Montreal, PQ H2Y 3R7

Pelletier, Gérard
former federal Liberal
Cabinet Minister from Quebec
c/o CECI
180 rue Ste-Catherine est
Montreal, PQ H2X 1K9

Pelletier, Jean
Chief of Staff, Prime Minister's Office/former mayor of Quebec
c/o Prime Minister's Office
80 Wellington St.
Ottawa, ON K1A 0A2

Pelletier, Marie Denise
popular singer
C.P. 246, Succ. Rosemont
Montreal, PQ H1X 3B6

Peltier, Jerry
Mohawk Chief, Kanesatake
P.O. Box 607
Kanesatake, PQ J0N 1E0

PEN Canada
Alison Gordon, President
international writers' lobby
24 Ryerson Ave.
Toronto, ON M5T 2P3

Penikett, Antony "Tony"
Premier of Yukon
P.O. Box 2703
Whitehorse, YK Y1A 2C6

Penner, Fred
children's singer/songwriter
108, 93 Lombard Ave.
Winnipeg, MB R3B 3B1

People, Words & Change/ Monde de Mots
Phil Jenkins, Co-ordinator
adult literacy organization
#210, 297 Sunnyside Ave.
Ottawa, ON K1S 0R9

Peoples Jewellers
Clare Copeland,
President and CEO
Canada's largest jewellers
1440 Don Mills Rd.
Toronto, ON M3B 3M1

Pepin, Jean-Luc
former federal Liberal
Cabinet Minister from Ontario
16 Rothwell Dr.
Gloucester, ON K1J 7G4

Pepsi-Cola Canada Beverages
Ron McEachern, President and CEO
1255 Bay St.
Toronto, ON M5R 2A9

Perley, E. Michael
environmentalist
401, 112 St. Clair Ave. W.
Toronto, ON M4V 2Y3

Perras, Anita *country singer*	c/o 5409 Eglinton Ave. W. Ste. 104 Etobicoke, ON M9C 5K6
Perreault, Raymond J. Liberal Senator from B.C.	Room 471-S The Senate Ottawa, ON K1A 0A4
Persons United for Self-Help (PUSH) Carol McGregor, Contact	597 Parliament St., #204 Toronto, ON M4X 1W3
Peterson, David R. former Premier of Ontario/*lawyer*	40 King St. W., Ste. 2100 Toronto, ON M5H 3C2
Peterson, Oscar *jazz pianist*	c/o Regal Recording Ltd. 2421 Hammond Rd. Mississauga, ON L5K 1T3
Peterson, Roy *editorial cartoonist*	c/o *Vancouver Sun* 2250 Granville St. Vancouver, BC V6H 3G2
Petrie, Anne host, Newsworld's "Petrie in Prime"	P.O. Box 2640 Calgary, AB T2P 2M7
Petrie, Daniel *TV and film director*	c/o Fred Specktor Creative Artists Agency 1888 Century Park E. Los Angeles, CA 90049 U.S.A.
Petro-Canada James M. Stanford President and CEO	P.O. Box 2844 Calgary, AB T2P 3E3
Petro-Canada International Peter M. Towe, Chairman	1601, 360 Albert St. Ottawa, ON K1R 7X7
Petten, William J. Liberal Senator from Newfoundland	Room 463-S The Senate Ottawa, ON K1A 0A4
Petty, Dini *talk show host*	c/o CTV P.O. Box 9, Stn. O Toronto, ON M4A 2M9

Pezim, Murray *stock promoter*/owner, B.C. Lions	c/o B.C. Lions 808 W. Hastings St. Vancouver, BC V6C 2X4
Philip, HRH Prince Duke of Edinburugh	Buckingham Palace London SW1, England
Phillips, Orville H. Liberal Senator from Newfoundland	Room 574-S The Senate Ottawa, ON K1A 0A4
Physicians for a **Smoke Free Canada** Dr. Mark C. Taylor, President	P.O. Box 4849, Ste. E Ottawa, ON K1S 5J1
Piche, Paul *singer*	c/o Spectra Scene 355 Ste-Catherine ouest, Ste. 700 Montreal, PQ H3B 1A5
Pickersgill, Jack former federal Liberal Cabinet Minister from Ontario	550 Maple Lane E. Rockcliffe Park Ottawa, ON K1M 0N6
Pilon, Daniel *actor*	c/o Triad 10100 Santa Monica Blvd. Los Angeles, CA 90067 U.S.A.
Pilon, Jean-Guy *author*	5724 Côte St-Antoine Montreal, PQ H4A 1R9
Pinel, Suzanne *children's entertainer/* *TV's* "Marie Soleil"	165–2111 Montreal Rd. Gloucester, ON K1J 8M8
Pinsent, Gordon *actor*	130 Carlton St., PH 8 Toronto, ON M5A 2K1
Pitfield, Michael Independent Senator from Ontario	Room 604-VB The Senate Ottawa, ON K1A 0A4
Plamondon, Luc *singer/songwriter*	c/o Editions Notation 2069 St. Denis St. Montreal, PQ H2X 3K8

Plan International Canada (formerly Foster Parents Plan) Paula McTavish, National Director	95 St. Clair Ave. W. Ste. 1001 Toronto, ON M4V 3B5
Planned Parenthood Federation of Canada Bonnie Johnson, Executive Director	#430, 1 Nicholas St. Ottawa, ON K1N 7B7
Plante, Jacques *first NHL goalie to use face mask*	c/o Hockey Hall of Fame BCE Place 30 Yonge St. Ottawa, ON M5E 1X8
Plummer, Amanda *actress*	15760 Ventura Blvd., #1730 Encino, CA 91436, U.S.A.
Plummer, Christopher *actor*	c/o Stanley Gorrie Whitson & Co. Cavendish Sq. London, England
Plumptre, Beryl *economist*	85 Lakeway Dr. Rockliffe Park Ottawa, ON K1L 5A9
Pocklington, Peter Chairman, Pocklington Financial Corp./owner, Edmonton Oilers Hockey Club	2500 Sun Life Place 10123 99 St. Edmonton, AB T5J 3H1
Podborski, Steve *ski champion*	Pod Enterprises Ltd. 294 Richmond St. E. Toronto, ON M5A 1P5
Pollution Probe Janine Ferretti, Executive Director *environmental lobby group*	12 Madison Ave. Toronto, ON M5R 2S1
Polanyi, Dr. John *Nobel Prize-winning chemist*	142 Collier St. Toronto, ON M4W 1M3
Pool, Léa *film director*	5964 rue Hutchison Outremont, PQ H2V 4C1
Potvin, Felix *hockey goalie*	c/o Toronto Maple Leafs 60 Carlton St. Toronto, ON M5B 1L1

Poulin, Bernard Aime
portrait artist
c/o Classic Perceptions
166 Heath St.
Ottawa, ON K1H 5E7

Prairie Oyster
rock group
c/o 77 Mowat Ave., Ste. 107
Toronto, ON M6K 3E3

Pratt, Christopher
artist/Newfoundland flag designer
P.O. Box 87, Mount Carmel
Mary's Bay, NF A0B 2M0

Pratt, Mary
artist
P.O. Box 87, Mount Carmel
Mary's Bay, NF A0B 2M0

PremierChoix: TVEC Inc.
Hubert Harel, President and CEO
French cable movie channel
2100 Ste-Catherine ouest
Ste. 800
Montreal, PQ H3H 2T3

Presbyterian Church in Canada
Rev. Linda Bell, Moderator
50 Wynford Dr.
Don Mills, ON M3C 1J7

Prévost, André
composer
227 av. Querles
Outremont, PQ H2V 3W1

Price Club Canada Inc.
Pierre Mignault,
President and CEO
wholesale warehouse chain
3000 Jacques Bureau
Laval, PQ H7P 5P7

Priestley, Jason
actor
c/o Beverly Hills, 90210
Fox Broadcasting Co.
10201 West Pico Blvd.
Los Angeles, CA 90035 U.S.A.

Prince Edward Island
Potato Museum
Dr. George Dewar, Director
P.O. Box 8
O'Leary, PE C0B 1V0

Pringle, Valerie
co-host, CTV's "Canada AM"
c/o CTV–Canada AM
P.O. Box 3000
Agincourt, ON M1S 3C6

Privy Council Office (PCO)
Glen Shortliffe, Clerk of the
Privy Council and Secretary to
the Cabinet
Langevin Block
80 Wellington St.
Ottawa, ON K1A 0A3

Probe International
Pat Adams
environmental advocacy group
225 Brunswick Ave.
Toronto, ON M5S 2M6

Progressive Conservative Party of Canada
Gerry St-Germain,
National President

200–161 Laurier Ave W.
Ottawa, ON K1P 5J2

Prophet, Ronnie
country singer

c/o 1030 17th Ave. S.
Nashville, TN 37212
U.S.A.

Provigo Inc.
Bertin Nadeau, Chairman
grocery chain

800 René Lévesque Blvd. W.
Suite 2600
Montreal, PQ H3B 1Y2

Prud'homme, Marcel
Independent Senator/former Liberal MP from Quebec

Room 624-VB
The Senate
Ottawa, ON K1A 0A4

Public Service Alliance of Canada (PSAC)
President, Daryl Bean
civil servants' union

233 Gilmour St.
Ottawa, ON K2P 0P1

Public Service Commission of Canada (PSC)
Robert J. Giroux, Chairman

300 Laurier Ave. W.
West Tower
Ottawa, ON K1A 0M7

Purdy, Albert (Al)
poet

R.R. #1
Ameliasburg, ON K0K 1A0

Pursuit of Happiness
rock band

192 Spadina Ave., Ste. 508
Toronto, ON M5V 2C2

Putting People First
Pat Thiessen,
Canadian Representative
organization that "supports the humane, ethical and responsible use of animals by mankind"

Blakely, P.O. Box 68031
Hamilton, ON L8M 3M7

PWA Corp.
Rhys T. Eyton,
President and CEO

700 2nd St. S.W.
Ste. 2800
Calgary, AB T2P 2W2

Q

"Write out of love; write out of instinct;
write out of reason."

Louis Untermeyer

Quaker Oats Co. of Canada, Ltd. Jon K. Grant, Chairman and CEO	Quaker Park, P.O. Box 4100 Peterborough, ON K9B 7B2
Québec dans le monde Denis Turcotte, Director *promotes Quebec abroad*	C.P. 8503 Ste-Foy, PQ G1V 4N5
Québec Nordiques Pierre Page, General Manager	Colisée de Québec 2205 av. du Colisée Quebec, PQ G1L 4W7
Quebec Winter Carnival/ Carnaval de Québec Michel Proulx, Director	290 rue Joly Quebec, PQ G1L 1N8
Queens University William C. Leggett, President	Room 206 Richardson Hall Kingston, ON K7L 3N6
Quilico, Louis *opera singer*	31 Claver Ave. Toronto, ON M6B 2V7

R

"The pen is the tongue of the hand—a silent utterer of words for the eye."

Henry Ward Beecher

Rabinovitch, Robert (Bob)
former federal civil servant
c/o Calridge Inc.
1170 Peel St.
Montreal, PQ H3B 4P2

Radio Canada International
Terry Hargreaves,
Executive Director
P.O. Box 6000
Montreal, PQ H3C 3A8

Radwanski, George
author/Publisher-in-Chief,
The Toronto Star
62 Cheritan Ave.
Toronto, ON M4R 1S6

Rae, Bob
Premier of Ontario
Premier's Office, Queen's Park
Toronto, ON M7A 1A2

Raffi (Raffi Cavoukian)
children's singer/environmental activist
c/o 129 West 69th St.
New York, NY 10023
U.S.A.

Raginsky, Nina
photographer
R.R. #2, Beddis Rd.
Compartment #7
Ganges, BC V0S 1E0

The Rankin Family
folk group
c/o Brook Diamond Productions
1819 Granville St., 4th fl.
Halifax, NS B3J 3R1

Rapoport, Anatol
author/professor of peace studies
University College
University of Toronto
Toronto, ON M5S 1A1

Rasky, Harry
film director
c/o CBC
P.O. Box 500, Stn. A
Toronto, ON M5W 1E6

Rasminsky, Louis
former Governor, Bank of Canada
1006–20 The Driveway
Ottawa, ON K2P 1C8

Read, Ken
Olympic gold medal skier
3806 Fifth St. S.W.
Calgary, AB T2S 2C8

Reader's Digest Association (Canada) Ltd.
Ralph Hancox, President and CEO
215 Redfern Ave.
Montreal, PQ H3Z 2V9

R.E.A.L. Women (Realistic Equal Active for Life Women)
Cecilia Forsyth, National President
P.O. Box 8813, Stn. T
Ottawa, ON K1G 3J1

Rebick, Judy
feminist/former President of N.A.C.
271 Spadina Rd.
Toronto, ON M5R 2V3

The Red Green Show
Steve Smith's TV comedy show
c/o CFPL Broadcasting Ltd.
P.O. Box 2880
London, ON N6A 4H9

Reeves, Hubert
astrophysicist
Batiment 28
91191 Gif-sur-Yvette, France

Regan, Gerald
former Premier of Nova Scotia and federal Liberal Cabinet Minister
P.O. Box 828, Stn. B
Ottawa, ON K1P 5P9

Reichmann Brothers
(Albert, Paul, and Ralph)
real estate developers
c/o Reichmann International
2 First Canadian Place
Toronto, ON M5X 1B5

Reid, Angus Darryl Bricker
pollster
1199 W. Hastings Ave., 11th fl.
Vancouver, BC V6E 3T5

Reid, Bill
Haida sculptor/printmaker
319–2890 Point Grey Rd.
Vancouver, BC V6K 1A9

Reid, Escott Meredith
former diplomat
R.R. #2, Ste-Cecile-de-Masham
PQ J0X 2W0

Reid, Fiona
actress
c/o Oscars & Abrams
59 Berkeley St.
Toronto, ON M5A 2W5

Reimer, Jan
Mayor of Edmonton
10015–103rd Ave.
Edmonton, AB T5J 0H1

Reisman, Sol
Canada-U.S. free trade negotiator
1611–50 O'Connor St.
Ottawa, ON K1P 6L2

Reitman, Ivan
film producer/director
c/o Universal St.udios
100 Universal City Plaza
Universal City, CA 91608, U.S.A.

Rekert, Winston
"Street Legal" *actor*
c/o CBC–Street Legal
P.O. Box 500, Stn. A
Toronto, ON M5W 1E6

Religious Society of Friends (Quakers)
Elaine Bishop, Co-ordinator
60 Lowther Ave.
Toronto, ON M5R 1C7

Reno, Ginette
singer
c/o Editions Notation
2069 St. Denis St.
Montreal, PQ H2X 3K8

Results/Résultats Canada
Jean-François Tardif,
National Director
International citizens' advocacy group that wants to eliminate causes of poverty
336, Place des Sorbiers
Hull, PQ J8Y 6R1

Retail Council of Canada
Alasdair McKichan, President
210 Dundas St. W., #600
Toronto, ON M5G 2E8

Rhéaume, Manon
first woman to play in an NHL game (1992)
c/o Knoxville Cherokees
500 E. Church St.
Knoxville, TN 37915, U.S.A.

Ricci, Nino
author
1–123 Huron St.
Toronto, ON M5T 2B3

Richard, Henri
hockey great,
"The Pocket Rocket"
c/o Hockey Hall of Fame
BCE Place, 30 Yonge St.
Toronto, ON M5E 1X8

Richard, Maurice "Rocket"
hockey legend
c/o Hockey Hall of Fame
BCE Place, 30 Yonge St.
Toronto, ON M5E 1X8

Richard III Society of Canada
Noreen Armstrong, Secretary
331 Rose Park Dr.
Toronto, ON M4T 1R8

Richards, David Adams
author
c/o McClelland & Stewart
481 University Ave., Ste 900
Toronto, ON M5G 2E9

Richler, Daniel
author/former Creative Head, Adult Arts Programming, TVO

c/o McClelland & Stewart
481 University Ave., Ste. 900
Toronto, ON M5G 2E9

Richler, Mordecai
author

1321 Sherbrooke St. W.
Apt. 80C
Montreal, PQ H3G 1J4

Riel, Maurice
Liberal Senator from Quebec

Room 265-EB
The Senate
Ottawa, ON K1A 0A4

Rinaldo, Sandie
CTV News anchor

c/o CTV
P.O. Box 3000
Agincourt, ON M1S 3C6

Riopelle, Jean-Paul
artist

10 rue Fremincourt
Paris 75015, France

Ritchie, Charles
author/former diplomat

216 Metcalfe St.
Ottawa, ON K2P 1R1

Ritchie, Gordon
Deputy Chief Canada-US Free Trade Negotiator

45 O'Connor St., Ste. 310
Ottawa, ON K1P 1A4

Ritter, Erika
author/broadcaster

c/o Playwrights Union of Canada
54 Wolseley St.
Toronto, ON M5C 1A5

Rivard, Michel
rock singer

c/o Spectra Scene
355 Ste-Catherine ouest
Ste. 700
Montreal, PQ H3B 1A5

Rivest, Jean Claude
Conservative Senator from Quebec

Room 602-VB
The Senate
Ottawa, ON K1A 0A4

Rizzuto, Pietro
Liberal Senator from Quebec

Room 579-F
The Senate
Ottawa, ON K1A 0A4

Road to Avonlea Fan Club

253 College St., Ste. 304
Toronto, ON M5T 1R5

Robbie, Roderick
Toronto SkyDome architect

Robbie Architects Inc.
11 Soho St., Ste. 204
Toronto, ON M5T 1Z6

Roberge, Fernand
Conservative Senator from Quebec
Room 601-VB
The Senate
Ottawa, ON K1A 0A4

Robertson, Brenda M.
Conservative Senator from New Brunswick
Room 401-VB
The Senate
Ottawa, ON K1A 0A4

Robertson, Gordon
former federal public servant
20 Westward Way
Rockcliffe Park
Ottawa, ON K1L 5A7

Robertson, Heather
author/journalist
175 Sherwood Ave.
Toronto, ON M4P 2A9

Robertson, Lloyd
CTV National News anchor
c/o CTV National News
P.O. Box 3000
Agincourt, ON M1S 3B6

Robertson, Robbie
rock singer/songwriter
c/o 955 S. Carrillo Dr., 3rd fl.
Los Angeles, CA 90048, U.S.A.

Robichaud, Hédard-J.
former Senator and Lieutenant Governor of New Brunswick
202 Blanchard St.
Caraquet, NB E0B 1K0

Robichaud, Louis J.
Liberal Senator/former Premier of New Brunswick
Room 266-EB
The Senate
Ottawa, ON K1A 0A4

Robinette, John Josiah
lawyer
P.O. Box 48
Toronto-Dominion Centre
Toronto, ON M5K 1E6

Robinson, Larry
former hockey player/ hockey official
c/o New Jersey Devils
Brendan Byrne Arena, Box 504
East Rutherford, NJ 07073, U.S.A.

Roblin, Duff
former Conservative Senator and Premier of Manitoba
977 Century Blvd.
Winnipeg, MB R3H 0W4

Roche, Douglas
former Canadian Ambassador for Disarmament
8923 Strathearn Dr.
Edmonton, AB T6C 4C8

Rock, Allan
federal Liberal Cabinet Minister from Newfoundland
Room 448–CB
House of Commons
Ottawa, ON K1A 0A6

Rogers, Garnet
folk singer
c/o James Fleming
733 North Main St.
Ann Arbor, MI 48104, U.S.A.

Rogers, Ted
President and CEO, Rogers Communications Inc.
P.O. Box 249
Toronto-Dominion Centre
Toronto, ON M5K 1J5

Rohmer, Richard
author/retired Major General
P.O. Box 129
Collingwood, ON L9Y 3Z4

Rolls-Royce Industries Canada Inc.
John P. Cheffins,
President and CEO
10 Carlson Court, Ste. 200
Rexdale, ON M9W 6L2

Romanow, Roy
Premier of Saskatchewan
Premier's Office
Legislative Building
Regina, SK S4S 0B3

Romper Room
children's TV show
c/o YTV
64 Jefferson Ave., Unit 18
Toronto, ON M6K 3H3

Ronald McDonald Children's Charities of Canada
Heather Clark, Administrator
c/o McDonald's Restaurants of Canada
McDonald's Place
Toronto, ON M3C 3L4

Roots Canada
Don Green and Michael Budman, co-founders
1162 Caledonia Rd.
Toronto, ON M6A 2W5

Rose, Paul
union activist/FLQ kidnapper
c/o CSN, Conseil Central
Montréal Metropolitain
1601 de Lorimier
Montreal, PQ H2K 4M5

Rosen, Harry
Chairman and CEO,
Harry Rosen Inc.
upscale men's clothing chain
11 Adelaide St. W.
Ste. 200
Toronto, ON M5H 3Y2

Rossiter, Eileen
Conservative Senator from P.E.I.
Room 402-VB, The Senate
Ottawa, ON K1A 0A4

Rostad, Wayne
host, "On the Road Again"
R.R. #1
Pakenham, ON K0A 2X0

Roux, Jean-Louis
actor/writer/director

2–4145 Blueridge Cres.
Montreal, PQ H3H 1S7

Rowat, Donald C.
ombudsman expert

Dept. of Political Science
Carleton University
Ottawa, ON K1S 5B6

Rowe, William (Bill)
political commentator/former Newfoundland Liberal Leader

P.O. Box 5007
St. John's, NF A1C 5V3

Rowlands, June
Mayor of Toronto

City Hall
100 Queen St. W.
Toronto, ON M5H 2N2

Roy, Bernard A.
former Principal Secretary to the Prime Minister

c/o Ogilvy Renault
1981 McGill College Ave.
Ste. 1100
Montreal, PQ H3A 3C1

Roy, Patrick
hockey goalie

c/o Montreal Canadiens
2313 rue Ste-Catherine ouest
Montreal, PQ H3H 1N2

Royal Bank of Canada
Allan Taylor, Chairman and CEO
Canada's largest bank

1 Place Ville Marie
Ste. 100
Montreal, PQ H3C 3A9

Royal Canadian Academy of the Arts
Bruce LeDain, President

900 Dufferin St., Ste. 201
Toronto, ON M6H 4B1

Royal Canadian Air Farce
comedy quartet

c/o CBC Radio
P.O. Box 500, Stn. A
Toronto, ON M5W 1E6

Royal Canadian Geographical Society
James W. Maxwell,
Executive Director

39 McArthur Ave.
Vanier, ON K1L 8L7

Royal Canadian Golf Association
Stephen D. Ross,
Executive Director

Golf House
R.R. #2
Oakville, ON L6J 4Z3

Royal Canadian Legion
Fred Hannigton,
Dominion Secretary

359 Kent St.
Ottawa, ON K2P 0R7

Royal Canadian Mint M.A. Lafontaine, Master of the Mint and President	320 Sussex Dr. Ottawa, ON K1A 0G8
Royal Canadian Mounted Police (RCMP) Norman Inkster, Commissioner	1200 Vanier Pkwy. Ottawa, ON K1A 0R2
Royal Canadian Mounted Police Museum Malcolm Wake, Director	P.O. Box 6500 Regina, SK S4P 3J7
Royal College of Physicians and Surgeons of Canada Gilles D. Hurteau, Executive Director	74 Stanley Ave. Ottawa, ON K1M 1P4
The Royal Conservatory of Music Peter Simon, President	273 Bloor St. W. Toronto, ON M5S 1W2
Royal LePage Ltd. Gordon C. Gray, Chairman	33 Yonge St., Ste. 1000 Toronto, ON M5E 1S9
Royal Military College of Canada J.B. Plant, Principal	Kingston, ON K7K 5L0
Royal Newfoundland Constabulary E.J. Coady, Chief of Police	P.O. Box 7247, Stn. C St. John's, NF A1E 3Y4
Royal Ontario Museum (ROM) John McNeill, Director	100 Queen's Park Toronto, ON M5S 2C6
The Royal Society of Canada John Meisel, President *promotes learning and research in the arts and sciences*	P.O. Box 9734 Ottawa, ON K1G 5J4
Royal Trustco Ltd. James Miller, CEO	P.O. Box 7500, Stn. A Toronto, ON M5W 1P9
Royal Winnipeg Ballet William Riske, General Manager	380 Graham Ave. Winnipeg, MB R3C 4K2
Rozema, Patricia *film producer/director*	20 Borden St. Toronto, ON M5S 2M9

Rubbo, Michael Datillo
film director

719 de L'Epee
Outremont, PQ H2V 3V1

Rubes, Jan
actor/opera singer/film director

44 Charles St. W., Apt. 2813
Toronto, ON M4Y 1R7

Rubinek, Saul
actor

c/o Great North Artists
350 Dupont St.
Toronto, ON M5R 1V9

Ruby, Clayton
criminal lawyer/co-founder, NORML Canada

Ruby and Edwardh
11 Prince Arthur Ave.
Toronto, ON M5R 1B2

Rule, Jane
author

The Fork Route 1
Galiano, BC V0N 1P0

Rural Dignity of Canada
Cynthia Patterson, National Co-ordinator
promotes quality of life in rural communities and the understanding of rural issues

P.O. Box 70
Barachois-de-Malbaie, PQ
G0C 1A0

Rush
rock group

c/o S.R.O.
189 Carlton St.
Toronto, ON M5A 2K7

Russel, Peter
constitutional affairs expert

14 Wychwood Park
Toronto, ON M6G 2V5

Ryan, Claude
Quebec Cabinet Minister/former Quebec Liberal Leader

20 Chauveau Ave., 3rd fl.
Quebec, PQ G1R 4J3

Rybczynski, Witold
architect/author

The Boathouse
206 Covey Hill
Hemmingford, PQ H3A 2K6

Ryckman, Larry
stock promoter/owner, Calgary Stampeders football club

c/o Calgary Stampeders
1817 Crowchild Trail N.W.
Calgary, AB T2M 4R6

Ryerson Polytechnic University
Terry Grier, President

350 Victoria St.
Toronto, ON M5B 2K3

S

"It takes two to write a letter as much as it takes two to make a quarrel."

Elizabeth Drew

Safdie, Moshe *architect*	100 Properzi Way Somerville, MA 02143 U.S.A.
Safer, Morley host, CBS's "60 Minutes"	c/o CBS 51 W. 52nd St. New York, NY 10019, U.S.A.
Saila, Pauta *Inuit sculptor*	Cape Dorset, NT X0A 0C0
St. Francis Xavier University David Lawless, President	Antigonish, NS B2G 1C0
St. Germain, Gerry Conservative Senator from B.C.	Room 205-VB The Senate Ottawa, ON K1A 0A4
Saint Jean Baptiste Society/ **Société Saint-Jean-Baptiste** Jean Dorion, President	82 rue Sherbrooke ouest Montreal, PQ H2X 1X3
St. John Ambulance D.J. Phillips, Secretary and CEO	312 Laurier Ave. E. Ottawa, ON K1N 8V4
St. Lawrence Seaway Authority Glendon R. Stewart, President and CEO	1400, 360 Albert St. Ottawa, ON K1R 7X7
Saint Mary's University Kenneth L. Ozman, President	Halifax, NS B3H 3C3

Saint Pierre, Marie
fashion designer
4455 rue St. Denis
Montreal, PQ H2J 2L2

Sainte Marie, Buffy
popular singer
c/o Management Network
3575 Cahuenga, Ste. 450
Los Angeles, CA 90068
U.S.A.

Salutin, Rick
author/journalist
350 Markham St.
Toronto, ON M6G 2K9

Salvation Army in Canada
Commissioner Wesley Harris,
Territorial Commander
P.O. Box 4021, Stn. A
Toronto, ON M5W 2B1

Sanger, Clyde
international affairs expert
200, 55 Murray St.
Ottawa, ON K1N 5M3

Santa Claus
(and Mrs. Claus)
The North Pole
H0H 0H0

Sapp, Allen
Native artist
2429 11th Ave.
Regina, SK S4P 0K4

Sarlos, Andrew
investment expert
Andrew Sarlos and Assoc. Ltd.
P.O. Box 51, T-D Tower
Toronto-Dominion Centre
Toronto, ON M5K 1E7

Saskatchewan Roughriders Football Club
Al Ford, General Manager
2940 10th Ave., Box 1277
Regina, SK S4P 3B8

Saskatchewan Telecommunications (SaskTel)
Fred Van Parys,
President and CEO
2121 Saskatchewan Dr.
Regina, SK S4P 3Y2

The Satellites
reggae band
1971 Spruce Hill Rd.
Pickering, ON L1V 1S6

***Saturday Night* magazine**
John Fraser, Editor
184 Front St., Ste. 400
Toronto, ON M5A 4N3

Saul, John Ralston
author
61 Hazelton Ave.
Toronto, ON M5R 2E3

Savage, John
Premier of Nova Scotia
Province House
Halifax, NS B3J 2T3

Save the Children Canada Leane Blank, National Director	3080 Yonge St., Ste. 6020 Toronto, ON M4N 9Z9
Sawatsky, John *journalist/author*	475 Bay St. Ottawa, ON K1R 6A7
Scarfe, Alan *actor/director*	21452 Encina Rd. Topanga, CA 90290 U.S.A.
Schafer, R. Murray *composer/author*	Box 425, Stn. K Toronto, ON M4P 2C9
Schibli, Paul *animation film director*	6 Hamilton Ave. N., 2nd fl. Ottawa, ON K1Y 4R1
Schlesinger, Joe *CBC journalist*	c/o CBC News Ottawa P.O. Box 3220, Stn. C Ottawa, ON K1Y 1E4
Schreyer, Edward former Governor General and Premier of Manitoba	Box 8 GR. 319 R.R. #3 Winnipeg, MB R3C 2E7
Scott, Camilla *actress*	c/o Creative Trust Int'l. 500A Bloor St. W. Toronto, ON M5S 1Y3
Scott, Cynthia *film director*	c/o NFB P.O. Box 6100 Montreal, PQ H3C 3H5
Scott-King, Barbara Ann *Olympic skating champion* "Canada's Sweetheart"	c/o Tom King SEAY Thomas Inc. 303 E. Wacker Dr., 20th fl. Chicago, IL 60601, U.S.A.
Scouts Canada Bill Wyman, President	1345 Baseline Rd. Ottawa, ON K2C 3G7
Scully, Robert host, CBC's "Venture" and Radio-Canada's "Scully Rencontre"	Case 98 place du Parc Montreal, PQ H2W 2M9
Seaborn, Blair *former federal public servant*	79 Mackay St. Ottawa, ON K1M 2E4
Sears Canada Inc. Donald Shaffer, President and CEO	222 Jarvis St. Toronto, ON M5B 2B8

Second City
Sally Cochrane, Producer
comedy revue theatre

The Old Firehall
110 Lombard St.
Toronto, ON M5C 1M3

Security Intelligence Review Committee
John Bassett, Chairman

P.O. Box 2430, Stn. D
Ottawa, ON K1P 5W5

Segal, Hugh
Conservative Party adviser

School of Policy Studies
Queen's University
Kingston, ON K7L 3N6

Seguin, Richard
singer

c/o Distribution Select
500 Ste-Catherine est
Montreal, PQ H2L 2C6

The Senate of Canada
"The Chamber of Sober, Second Thought"

Parliament Buildings
Wellington St.
Ottawa, ON K1A 0A4

Sex Information and Education Council of Canada (SIECCAN)
Michael Barrett, Chairperson

850 Coxwell Ave.
East York, ON M4C 5R1

Seymour, Lynn
ballerina/choreographer

c/o Artists in Action
16 Balderton St.
London W1Y 1TF, England

Shack, Eddie
former hockey player

686 Oriole Pkwy.
Toronto, ON M4R 2C5

Shadbolt, Jack
artist

5121 Harborview Rd.
North Burnaby, BC V5B 1C9

Shaffer, Paul
*composer/*leader, CBS Big Band

c/o CBS–Late Show with David Letterman
524 West 57th St.
New York, NY 10019
U.S.A.

Sharon, Lois and Bram
children's musical trio

c/o 24 Ryerson Ave., 4th fl.
Toronto, ON M5T 2P3

Sharp, Mitchell
former federal Liberal
Cabinet Minister from Ontario

33 Monkland Ave.
Ottawa, ON K1S 1Y8

Shatner, William *Star Trek*'s "Captain Kirk"	c/o Larry Thompson 1440 S. Sepulueda Blvd. Ste. 118 Los Angeles, CA U.S.A.
Shaver, Helen *actress*	c/o Oscars and Abrams 59 Berkeley St. Toronto, ON M5A 2W5
Shaw Cablesystems Ltd. James R. Shaw, President, Chairman, and Director	7605 50 St. Edmonton, ON T6B 2W9
Shaw Festival Theatre Foundation Elaine Calder, Administrative Director	P.O. Box 774 Niagara-on-the-Lake, ON L0S 1J0
Shebib, Donald *film producer/director*	312 Wright Ave. Toronto, ON M6R 1L9
Shell Canada Ltd. J.M. (Jack) MacLeod, President and CEO	P.O. Box 100, Stn. M Calgary, AB T2P 2H5
Shields, Carol *author*	237 Wellington Cres., Ste. 701 Winnipeg, MB R3M 0A1
Shimkus, Joanna *actress*	c/o Verdon Productions 310 9350 Wilshire Blvd. Beverly Hills, CA 90212, U.S.A.
Shirley Solomon *TV talk show host*	c/o The Shirley Show 43 Front St. E., 3rd fl. Toronto, ON M5E 1B3
SHL Systemhouse Inc. John Oltman, CEO	50 O'Connor St., Ste. 1616 Ottawa, ON K1P 6L2
Shoppers Drug Mart Ltd. David R. Bloom, Chairman and CEO	225 Yorkland Blvd. Willowdale, ON M2J 4Y7
Short, Martin *actor/comedian*	c/o 9830 Wilshire Blvd. Beverly Hills, CA 90212 U.S.A.

Shoyama, Thomas Kunito *former federal public servant*	3030 Midland Rd. Victoria, BC V8R 6P1
Shulman, Dr. Morton *physician/author/*founder, Dephrenyl Research Ltd.	378 Roncesvalles Ave. Toronto, ON M6R 2M7
Shuster, Frank *comedian*	c/o CBC P.O. Box 500, Stn. A Toronto, ON M5W 1E6
Siberry, Jane *rock singer*	P.O. Box 291 238 Davenport Rd. Toronto, ON M5R 1J6
Sierra Club of Canada Elizabeth May, National Representative	#420, 1 Nicholas St. Ottawa, ON K1N 7B7
Sigler, John H. *Middle East expert*	Dept. of Political Science Carleton University 1125 Colonel By Dr. Ottawa, ON K1S 5B6
Simard, Jean-Maurice Conservative–Independent Senator from Quebec	Room 622-VB The Senate Ottawa, ON K1A 0A4
Simard, Natalie *rock singer*	2322 Sherbrooke St. E. Montreal, PQ H2K 1E5
Simard, René *rock singer*	2322 Sherbrooke St. E. Montreal, PQ H2K 1E5
Simms, Len Newfoundland Conservative Leader	Confederation Bldg. P.O. Box 8700 St. John's, NF A1B 4J6
Simon, Mary President, Inuit Circumpolar Conference	515–170 Laurier Ave. W. Ottawa, ON K1P 5V5
Simon Fraser University John O. Stubbs, President	Burnaby, BC V5A 1S6
Simpson, Jeffrey columnist, *The Globe and Mail*	165 Sparks St., 3rd fl. Ottawa, ON K1P 5B9

Sinclair, Lister
host, CBC's "Ideas"

c/o CBC–Ideas
P.O. Box 500, Stn. A
Toronto, ON M5W 1E6

Sirois, Charles
President, Téléglobe Inc.

1000 de la Gauchetière ouest
Montreal, PQ H3B 4X5

Skvorecky, Josef
author/professor

Dept. of English
Erindale College
University of Toronto
Mississauga, ON L5L 1C6

Slade, Bernard
TV and stage playwright

1262 Lago Vista Place
Beverly Hills, CA 90210
U.S.A.

Slater, Gordon
Dominion Carilloneur of Canada

House of Commons
Ottawa, ON K1A 0A6

Sloan
rock group

c/o The Agency
41 Britain St., Ste. 200
Toronto, ON M5A 1R7

Slonim, Rabbi Reuben
President, Association for the Living Jewish Spirit

625 Roselawn Ave.
Toronto, ON M5N 1K7

Small, Doug
broadcaster/journalist

c/o *The Ottawa Sun*
380 Hunt Club Rd.
Ottawa, ON K1G 5H7

Smart, Patricia
author

11 Regent St.
Ottawa, ON K1S 4R4

Smee, Doug
Canadian Executive Director on the International Monetary Fund (IMF)

IMF
700 19th St.
Washington, DC 20431
U.S.A.

Smillie, Robert Ian
international development consultant

618 Melbourne Ave.
Ottawa, ON K2A 1X1

Smith, Arnold Cantwell
*former diplomat/*first Secretary General of the Commonwealth

260 Metcalfe St., #4B
Ottawa, ON K2P 1R6

Smith, Lois
ballerina/choreographer

s15 c12, R.R. #4
Gibsons, BC V0N 1V0

Smith, Michael *Nobel Prize-winning chemist*	Biotechnology Lab Room 237, Wesbrook Bldg. University of British Columbia 6174 University Blvd. Vancouver, BC V6T 1W5
Smith, Ray *author*	c/o The Writers' Union of Canada 24 Ryerson Ave. Toronto, ON M5T 2P3
E.D. Smith & Sons Ltd. Ernest L.G. Smith, Chairman	Highway #8 Winona, ON L0R 2L0
Smits, Sonja *actress*	c/o Great North Artists Mgmt. 350 Dupont St. Toronto, ON M5R 1V9
Smokers' Freedom Society Phil Gillies, President	250 The Esplanade, #306 Toronto, ON M5A 1J2
SNC Group Inc. Guy Saint-Pierre, Chairman *consulting engineering company*	2 Place Felix-Martin Montreal, PQ H2Z 1Z3
Sniderman, Sam "Sam the Record Man"	274 Church St. Toronto, ON M5B 1Z5
Snow (Darrin O'Brien) *rap singer*	c/o The Agency 41 Britain St., Ste. 200 Toronto, ON M5A 1R7
Snow, Hank *country singer*	310 E. Marthonna Dr. Madison, TN 37115, U.S.A.
Snow, Michael *artist/photographer/filmmaker*	176 Cottingham St. Toronto, ON M4V 1C5
Snowbirds Canadian Forces Air Demonstration Squadron Maj. Dean Rainkie, Squadron Commander	431 Air Demonstration Squadron CFB Moose Jaw P.O. Box 5000 Moose Jaw, SK S6H 7Z8
Sobey, Donald R. Chairman and Director, Sobey's Inc. *Maritime grocery chain*	115 King St. Stellarton, NS B0K 1S0
Socialist Party of Canada Steve Szalai, General Secretary	P.O. Box 4280 Victoria, BC V8X 3X8

Société Radio-Canada (SRC)
CBC's French-language network
C.P. 6000, succ. Centre Ville
Montreal, PQ H3C 3A8

Society of Composers, Authors and Music Publishers of Canada (SOCAN)
Mark Altman, President
41 Valleybrook Dr.
Don Mills, ON M3B 2S6

Solway, Larry
broadcast journalist
217 Old Forest Hill Rd.
Toronto, ON M6C 2H2

Somain, Jean-Francois
(alias J.F. Somcynsky)
author/diplomat
Canada Court
2401, 7-3-24 Akasaka
Minato-Ku, Tokyo 107, Japan

Sopinka, John
Justice, Supreme Court of Canada
Supreme Court of Canada
Wellington St.
Ottawa, ON K1A 0J1

Souster, Raymond
poet
39 Baby Point Rd.
Toronto, ON M6S 2G2

Southam Business Communications Inc.
William E. Ardell,
President and CEO
Canada's largest newspaper publisher
1450 Don Mills Rd.
Don Mills, ON M3B 2X7

Spar Aerospace Ltd.
John D. MacNaughton,
President and CEO
Canadarm developer
5090 Explorer Dr.
Ste. 900
Mississauga, ON L4W 4X6

Sparrow, Herbert
Liberal Senator from Saskatchewan
Room 261-E
The Senate
Ottawa, ON K1A 0A4

Spector, Norman
Ambassador to Israel/former Prime Ministerial Chief of Staff
P.O. Box 500 (Tel Aviv)
Stn. A
Ottawa, ON K1N 8T7

Spicer, Keith
Chairman, Canadian Radio-Television and Telecommunications Commission (CRTC)
The CRTC
Ottawa, ON K1A 0N2

Spirit of the West
rock band
777 Prior St.
Vancouver, BC V6A 2G8

Spivak, Mira
Conservative Senator from Manitoba

Room 903-VB
The Senate
Ottawa, ON K1A 0A4

Sports Federation of Canada
Margaret Barber, Executive Director
largest sports advocacy group

1600 James Naismith Dr.
Gloucester, ON K1B 5N4

Spremo, Boris
photographer

c/o *The Toronto Star*
One Yonge St.
Toronto, ON M5E 1E6

Stairs, Denis
Canadian foreign policy expert

4 Rockwood St.
Halifax, NS B3N 1X5

Stanbury, Richard
Liberal Senator from Ontario

Room 269-E
The Senate
Ottawa, ON K1A 0A4

Standards Council of Canada
Georges Archer, President

45 O'Connor St., Ste. 1200
Ottawa, ON K1P 6N7

Stanfield, Robert L.
former Leader, federal Conservative Party and Premier of Nova Scotia

136 Acacia Ave.
Rockcliffe Park
Ottawa, ON K1M 0R1

Stanfield's Ltd.
F. Thomas Stanfield, President and CEO
underwear manufacturer

P.O. Box 190
Truro, NS B2N 5C2

Stanley, George
designer of Canadian flag
former Lieutenant-Governor of New Brunswick

18 Pond Shore Rd.
P.O. Box 790
Sackville, NB E0A 3C0

Starnes, John
author/former diplomat
former Director General of RCMP Security Service

9–100 Rideau Terrace
Ottawa, ON K1M 0Z2

Statistics Canada
Ivan P. Fellegi, Chief Statistician of Canada

R.H. Coates Bldg.
Tunney's Pasture
Ottawa, ON K1A 0T6

Steele, Harry
President, Newfoundland Capital Corporation Ltd.

800 Windmill Rd., Ste. 302
Dartmouth, NS B3B 1L1

Stein, Janice
Middle East expert

University of Toronto
Political Science Dept.
100 St. George St., #3025
Toronto, ON M5S 1A1

Steinberg, David
comedian/actor

c/o William Morris Agency
151 El Camino
Beverley Hills, CA 90212
U.S.A.

Stelco Inc.
Frederick Telmer, Chairman
Canada's largest steel company

P.O. Box 2030
Hamilton, ON L8N 3T1

Stevens, Geoffrey
journalist

c/o *The Sun Times of Canada*
515 Bay St. W.
Tampa, FL 33606

Stevens, Sinclair
former federal Conservative Cabinet Minister from Ontario

R.R. #3
King City, ON L0G 1K0

Stevens, William
film producer/director/musician

P.O. Box 11069, Stn. H
Nepean, ON K2H 7T8

Stewart, John B.
Liberal Senator from Nova Scotia

Room 801-VB
The Senate
Ottawa, ON K1A 0A4

Stewart, Walter
journalist/author

Sturgeon Point, ON
K0M 1N0

Stojko, Elvis
figure skating champion

c/o Canadian Figure Skating Association
1600 James Naismith Dr.
Ste. 403
Gloucester, ON K1B 5N4

Stollery, Peter
Liberal Senator from Ontario

Room 216-EB
The Senate
Ottawa, ON K1A 0A4

Strange Advance
rock band

c/o Current Management
366 Adelaide St. E., #437
Toronto, ON M5A 3X9

Stratas, Teresa *opera singer*	c/o Metropolitan Opera Co. Lincoln Center Plaza New York, NY 10023, U.S.A.
Stratford Festival Gary Thomas, General Manager	55 Queen St. Stratford, ON N5A 4M9
Stratton, Terrance Conservative Senator from Manitoba	Room 902-VB The Senate Ottawa, ON K1A 0A4
Streit, Marlene Stewart *golf champion*	R.R. #4 Stouffville, ON L4H 7X5
Strong, Maurice Chairman, Ontario Hydro/*former international civil servant*	Ontario Hydro 700 University Ave. Toronto, ON M5G 1X6
Stulberg, Gordon President, Polygram Pictures Corp.	3940 Overland Ave. Culver City, CA 90230 U.S.A.
Stursberg, Peter *writer/broadcaster*	5132 Alderfield Pl. W. Vancouver, BC V7W 2W7
Sullivan, Kevin *TV/film producer*	c/o Sullivan Films 16 Clarence Square Toronto, ON M5V 1H1
Summers, Ken Commander, Canadian Forces, Operation Desert Storm	Canadian Defence Liaison Office 501 Pennsylvania Ave. N.W. Washington, DC 20001 U.S.A.
Sung, Alfred *fashion designer*	207 Queen's Quay W. Toronto, ON M5J 2P5
Sûreté du Québec Robert Levigne, Director *Quebec provincial police*	1701 rue Parthenais Montreal, PQ H2K 3S7
Surjik, Stephen *film director/*"Wayne's World 2"	15A Rusholme Dr. Toronto, ON M6J 3K1
Sutherland, Donald *actor*	c/o 760 N. La Cienega Blvd. Los Angeles, CA 90069 U.S.A.
Sutherland, Kiefer *actor*	c/o 9200 Sunset Blvd., #25 Los Angeles, CA 90069 U.S.A.

Suttles and Seawinds
Gary and Vicki Lynn Bardon,
(designers and founders)
Maritime clothing chain

466 Main St.
Mahone Bay, NS B0J 2E0

Suzuki, Dr. David
scientist/author

Dept. of Zoology
University of British Columbia
Vancouver, BC V6T 2A9

Swan, Susan
author

609 Logan Ave.
Toronto, ON M4K 3C2

Sylvain, John
Conservative Senator from
Quebec

Room 250-N
The Senate
Ottawa, ON K1A 0A4

Symphony Nova Scotia Society
Michael La Leune,
General Manager

1646 Barrington St.
Halifax, NS B3J 2A3

T

"I have only made this letter long because
I have not had time to make it shorter."

Blaise Pascal

Taillibert, Roger René Montreal Olympic Stadium *architect*	163 rue de la Pompe 75116 Paris, France
Tanobe, Miyuki *artist*	C.P. 33, Ste-Antoine-sur-Richelieu PQ, J0L 1R0
Tapp, Gordie *country musician*	c/o Mascioli Entertainment 11 Music Circle S. Nashville, TN 37203, U.S.A.
Tarzan Dan (Dan Freeman) host, YTV's "Hit List"/*announcer*	c/o YTV–Hit List 64 Jefferson Ave., #18 Toronto, ON M6K 3H3
Tascona, Antonio "Tony" *artist*	208 Provencher Blvd. Winnipeg, MB R2H 0G4
Tasse, Alain Quebec NDP Leader	410 rue Nicolas, Ste. 214 Montreal, PQ H2Y 2P5
Tata, Sam *photographer*	4361 Beaconsfield Ave. Montreal, PQ H4A 2H5
Taylor, Carol *broadcast journalist*	c/o CTV–Vancouver 1500 West Georgia St. Ste. 790 Vancouver, BC V6G 2Z5
Taylor, Charles P.B. *writer*	P.O. Box 67 Oshawa, ON L1H 7K8

Taylor, Ken
Iran hostage-caper diplomat
146 West 57 St.
New York, NY 10019, U.S.A.

Taylor, Richard
Nobel Prize-winning physicist
P.O. Box 4349, Mail Stop 96
Stanford, CA 94309, U.S.A.

Téléfilm Canada
Pierre Desrochers, Executive Director
600 de la Gauchetière W.
14th fl.
Montreal, PQ H3B 4L8

Télémedia
Philippe de Gaspé Beaubien, Chairman and CEO
1010 rue Sherbrooke ouest
Ste. 1610
Montreal, PQ H3A 2R7

Télévision Quatre Saisons
405 Ave. Ogilvy
Montreal, PQ H3H 2Y4

Telus Corporation
Hal M. Nelder, President
telecommunications company
10020-100 Street
Edmonton, AB T5J 0N3

Templeton, Charles
author/broadcaster
701 Don Mills Rd., Apt. 2600
Toronto, ON M3C 1R9

Tennant, Jan
first Canadian woman to anchor evening news on network television
130 Carlton St, Ste. 1404
Toronto, ON M5A 4K3

Tennant, Veronica
ballerina/writer
c/o The National Ballet of Canada
157 King St. E.
Toronto, ON M5C 1G9

Tennis Canada
(Canadian Tennis Association)
Bob Moffatt, President
3111 Steeles Ave. W.
Downsview, ON M3J 3H2

Tewksbury, Mark
Olympic gold medal swimmer
c/o Swimming Canada
1600 James Naismith Dr., Ste. 208
Gloucester, ON K1B 5N4

Thatcher, Colin
former Saskatchewan politician/ convicted murderer
c/o Edmonton Institution
P.O. Box 2290
Edmonton, AB T5J 3H7

Théâtre du Nouveau Monde
Olivier Reichenbach, Artistic Director
137, rue St-Ferdinand
Bureau 201,
Montreal, PQ H4C 2S7

Theriault, Norbert Liberal Senator from New Brunswick	Room 274-EB The Senate Ottawa, ON K1A 0A4
Thicke, Alan *actor/TV personality*	P.O. Box 724 Altadena, CA 91001 U.S.A.
Thiessen, Gordon Governor, Bank of Canada	234 Wellington St. Ottawa, ON K1A 0G9
***This Country Canada* magazine** Wayne Grady, Editor	P.O. Box 220 Dunrobin, ON K0A 1T0
This Hour Has 22 Minutes *TV comedy show*	c/o CBC P.O. Box 500, Stn. A Toronto, ON M5W 1E6
Thom, Linda M. *Olympic sport pistol* *gold medallist*	19–551 Riverdale Ave. Ottawa, ON K1S 1S3
Thomas, Audrey *author*	c/o The Writers' Union of Canada 24 Ryerson Ave. Toronto, ON M5T 2P3
Thomas, Peter founder, Century 21 Real Estate	700 West Georgia St. Ste. 2910 Vancouver, BC V7Y 1B6
Thompson, Andrew Liberal Senator from Ontario	Room 485-S The Senate Ottawa, ON K1A 0A4
Thomson, Lord Kenneth Chairman of the Board and Director, The Thomson Corp.	The Quadrangle P.O. Box 4YG 180 Wardour St. London W1A 4YG, England
Thomson, Murray M. *international disarmament expert* co-founder, Peacefund Canada	206, 145 Spruce St. Ottawa, ON K1R 6P1
Tilley, Alexander Founder and President, Tilley Endurables Inc.	900 Don Mills Rd. Don Mills, ON M3C 1V8

TIME Canada Elizabeth Valk Long, Publisher	175 Bloor St. E. North Tower, Ste. 602 Toronto, ON M4W 3R8
Timex Canada Inc. Patrick Morris, Chairman	445 Hood Rd. Markham, ON L3R 8H1
Tip Top Tailors Donald J. Evans, Chairman and CEO *men's clothing retail chain*	637 Lakeshore Blvd. W. Toronto, ON M5V 1A8
Tkachuk, David Conservative Senator from Saskatchewan/Chairman of the Diefenbaker Society	Room 809-VB The Senate Ottawa, ON K1A 0A4
Tobias, Ken *singer*	P.O. Box 609, Stn. F Toronto, ON M4Y 2L8
Tobin, Brian federal Liberal Cabinet Minister from Newfoundland	Room 807–CB House of Commons Ottawa, ON K1A 0A6
Too Many Cooks *rock band*	c/o Paul Matte 1445 Lambert-Closse Montreal, PQ H3H 1Z5
Tookoome, Simon *Inuit painter/sculptor*	c/o The Jessie Oonark Arts and Crafts Centre Baker Lake, NT X0C 0A0
Toronto Argonaut Football Club Bob O'Billovich, General Manager	Exhibition Stadium Toronto, ON M6K 3C3
Toronto Blue Jays Paul Beeston, President and CEO	300 The Esplanade W., Ste. 3200 Toronto, ON M5V 3B3
Toronto Dominion Bank Richard M. Thomson, Chairman and CEO	P.O. Box 1 Toronto-Dominion Centre Toronto, ON M5K 1A2
Toronto International Film Festival (formerly Festival of Festivals) Helga Stephenson, Executive Director	70 Carlton St. Toronto, ON M5B 1L6

***Toronto Life* magazine**
Shelagh Tarleton, Publisher
59 Front St. E.
Toronto, ON M5E 1B3

Toronto Maple Leafs
Cliff Fletcher, General Manager
Maple Leaf Gardens
60 Carlton St.
Toronto, ON M5B 1L1

Toronto Mendelssohn Choir
Michael Ridout, Manager
60 Simcoe St.
Toronto, ON M5J 2H5

Toronto Philharmonic Orchestra
35 McCaul St.
Toronto, ON M5T 1V7

The Toronto Star
David R. Jolley,
Publisher and President
Canada's largest newspaper
One Yonge St.
Toronto, ON M5E 1E6

Toronto Stock Exchange (TSE)
John Pearce Bunting,
President and CEO
The Exchange Tower
2 First Canadian Place
Toronto, ON M5X 1J2

The Toronto Sun
Jim Tighe, Publisher
333 King St. E.
Toronto, ON M5A 1A1

Toronto Symphony
J. Wray Armstrong,
Managing Director
60 Simcoe St.
Toronto, ON M5J 2H5

Towers, Gordon
Lieutenant Governor of Alberta
Legislature Building, 3rd fl.
Edmonton, AB T5K 2B6

Toyota Canada Inc.
Toshio Kunii, President
1291 Bellamy Rd. N.
Scarborough, ON M1H 1H9

Tracey Prescott and Lonesome Daddy
country music band
Clayton, ON K0A 1P0

Tracy, Paul
race car driving champion
20 Cosentino Dr.
Scarborough, ON M1P 3A2

Tragically Hip
rock band
c/o 68 Sparkhall Ave.
Toronto, ON M4K 1G6

TransCanada Pipelines
G.J. Maier, Chairman, CEO,
and President
P.O. Box 1000, Stn. M
Calgary, AB T2P 4K5

Transport 2000 Canada
Robert Evans, President
provides consumers with information on transportation issues

P.O. Box 858, Stn. B
Ottawa, ON K1P 5P9

Trebek, Alex
host, "Jeopardy!"

c/o Jeopardy!
1040 N. Las Palmas Ave.
Los Angeles, CA 90038-2489
U.S.A.

Tremaine, Don
former host,
"The Don Messer Show"

c/o CBC
P.O. Box 3000
Halifax, NS B3J 3E9

Tremblay, Michel
author/playwright

294 Carre St-Louis, 5e
Montreal, PQ H2X 1A4

Trent, John Elliot
political scientist

Political Science Dept.
University of Ottawa
Ottawa, ON K1N 6N5

Trent University
David Morrison, President

P.O. Box 4800
Peterborough, ON K9J 7B8

Trinity College
Robert H. Painter, Provost

6 Hoskin Ave.
Toronto, ON M5S 1H8

Triumph
rock band

3611 Mavis Rd., Unit 3
Mississauga, ON L5C 1T7

Trivial Pursuit
Chris Haney and Scott Abbot
inventors

Horn Abbot Ltd.
184 Pearl St., Ste. 301
Toronto, ON M5H 1L5

Trooper
rock band

244–1450 Johnston Rd.
White Rock, BC V4B 5E9

Trotter, Kate
actress

c/o Oscars and Abrams
59 Berkeley St.
Toronto, ON M5A 2W5

Trudeau, Pierre Elliott
former Liberal Prime Minister

c/o Heenan Blaikie
1250 boul. René-Lévesque ouest
Ste. 2500
Montreal, PQ H3B 4Y1

Trudeau-Kemper, Margaret
author/former TV host

95 Victoria St.
Ottawa, ON K1M 1S4

Trueman, Peter
broadcaster/journalist
R.R. #1
Stella, ON K0H 2S0

TSN (The Sports Network)
Gordon Craig, President
1155 Leslie St.
Don Mills, ON M3C 2J6

Tugwell, Maurice
terrorism expert/Director,
The Mackenzie Institute for the Study of Terrorism, Revolution and Propaganda
P.O. Box 338
Adelaide Postal Stn.
Toronto, ON M5C 2J4

Turner, John
former Liberal Prime Minister
c/o Miller Thomson
20 Queen St. W.
Box 27, Ste. 2700
Toronto, ON M5H 3S1

Turp, Daniel
Bloc Québécois adviser/TV commentator
c/o Bloc Québécois
425 de Maisonneuve ouest
14ème étage
Montréal, PQ H3A 3G5

TV Guide
John Keyes, Editor
50 Holly St.
Toronto, ON M4S 3B3

TVOntario (TVO)
Peter Herrndorf, Chairman and CEO
2180 Yonge St.
Toronto, ON M4S 2B9

Twinn, Walter P.
Conservative Senator from Alberta
Room 162-N
The Senate
Ottawa, ON K1A 0A4

Tyson, Ian
country singer
c/o Mascioli Entertainment
11 Music Circle S.
Nashville, TN 37203
U.S.A.

Tyson, Sylvia
country singer
c/o 77 Mowat Ave., Ste. 107
Toronto, ON M6K 3E3

U

"[Letter-writing]… a habit the pleasure of which increases with practice, but becomes more irksome with neglect."

Abigail Adams

UFO Centre
Henry H. McKay, Director
P.O. Box 54
Agincourt, ON M1S 3B4

Ultramar Canada Inc.
N. Di Tomaso, Chairman
petroleum company
2200 McGill College Ave.
Montreal, PQ H3A 3L3

Unger, Jim
"Herman" *cartoonist*
P.O. Box 10806
Nassau, Bahamas

UNICEF Canada
Harry S. Black,
Executive Director
443 Mt. Pleasant Rd.
Toronto, ON M4S 2L8

Unitarian Service Committee of Canada (USC)
John Martin, CEO
56 Sparks St.
Ottawa, ON K1P 5B1

United Empire Loyalists' Association of Canada
Dorothy Chisholm, Administrator
The George Brown House
50 Baldwin St.
Toronto, ON M5T 1L4

United Nations Association of Canada
Angus Archer,
Executive Director
808–63 Sparks St.
Ottawa, ON K1P 5A6

United Nations Centre for Human Settlements (Habitat)
130 Albert St., #417
Ottawa, ON K1P 5G4

United Nations peacekeeping operations in which Canadians serve:

■ Angola	CCUNAVEM (OP Pastel) Belleville, ON K0K 3R0
■ Cambodia	CO CDN Contingent UN Transitional Authority in Cambodia (CCUNTAC) CFPO 5050 Belleville, ON K0K 3R0
■ Egypt, Israel, Jordan, Syria	CCUNTSO CFPO 5002 Belleville, ON K0K 3R0
■ Egypt (Sinai)	CCMFO, Multinational Force and Observers APO New York, NY 09677-1200 U.S.A.
■ El Salvador	Contingente Canadiense Division Militar De Onusal Apartado Postal 2257 San Salvador, El Salvador
■ Iraq and Kuwait	CCUNIKOM CFPO 5006 Belleville, ON K0K 3R0
■ Somalia	CO CDN Contingent CFPO 5005 Belleville, ON K0K 3R0
■ Syria (Golan Heights)	CCUNDOF CFPO 5002 Belleville, ON K0K 3R0
■ Western Sahara	CCMINURSO CFPO 5047 Belleville, ON K0K 3R0
■ Yugoslavia	Canadian Contingent United Nations Protection Force (CCUNPROFOR) CFPO 5003 Belleville, ON K0K 3R0

United Way David Armour, President	56 Sparks St., Ste 404 Ottawa, ON K1P 5A9
Unitel Communications Inc. Stanley Lacks, President and CEO	200 Wellington St. W. Toronto, ON M5V 3C7
University of Alberta Paul Davenport, President	Room 3-1, University Hall Edmonton, AB T6G 2E1
University of British Columbia David Strangway, President	6328 Memorial Rd., Ste. 107 Vancouver, BC V6T 1Z2
University of Calgary F. Murray Fraser, President	2500 University Dr. N.W. Calgary, AB T2N 1N4
University of Guelph Mordechai Rozanski, President	Guelph, ON N1G 2W1
University of Manitoba Arnold Naimark, President	Winnipeg, MB R3T 2N2
University of New Brunswick Robin Armstrong, President	P.O. Box 4400 Fredericton, NB E3B 5A3
University of Ottawa Marcel Hamelin, Rector	P.O. Box 450, Stn. A Ottawa, ON K1N 6N5
University of Prince Edward Island C.W.J. Eliot, President	Charlottetown, PE C1A 4P3
University of Regina D.O. Wells, President	Regina, SK S4S 0A2
University of Saskatchewan George Ivany, President	Saskatoon, SK S7N 0W0
University of Toronto Robert S. Pritchard, President	27 Kings College Circle Toronto, ON M5S 1A1
University of Victoria David F. Strong, President	P.O. Box 1700 Victoria, BC V8W 2Y2
University of Waterloo James Downey, President	Waterloo, ON N2L 3G1
University of Western Ontario George K. Pedersen, President and Vice-Chancellor	London, ON N6A 3K7

University of Windsor
R.W. Ianni, President

401 Sunset Ave.
Windsor, ON N9B 3P4

University of Winnipeg
Marsha Hanen, President

515 Portage Ave.
Winnipeg, MB R3B 2E9

Urban Alliance on Race Relations
Fazela Haniff, Co-ordinator

#203, 675 King St. W.
Toronto, ON M5V 1M9

Urquhart, Jane
author

P.O. Box 208
Wellesley, ON N0B 2T0

UZEB
rock group

3575 boul. St-Laurent
Ste. 614
Montreal, PQ H2X 2T7

V

"Someone, somewhere, wants a letter from you."

British Post Office slogan

Vachon, Rogie *former hockey goalie/hockey executive*	c/o Los Angeles Kings 3900 W. Manchester Blvd. Inglewood, CA 90306 U.S.A.
Valdy *singer/songwriter*	151 Reynolds St. Fulford Harbour, Salt Spring Island, BC V0S 1C0
Vancouver Art Gallery William Holmes, Director	750 Hornby St. Vancouver, BC V6Z 2H7
Vancouver Canucks Pat Quinn, General Manager	Pacific Coliseum 100 N. Renfrew St. Vancouver, BC V5K 3N7
Vancouver Magazine John Keyes, Editor	555 W. 12th Ave. Ste. 300, S.E. Tower Vancouver, BC V5Z 4L4
Vancouver Stock Exchange (VSE) Donald J. Hudson, President	P.O. Box 10333 609 Granville St. Vancouver, BC V7Y 1H1
The Vancouver Sun Donald Babick, Publisher and President	2250 Granville St. Vancouver, BC V6H 3G2
Vanderhaeghe, Guy *author/playwright*	c/o The Writers' Union of Canada 24 Ryerson Ave. Toronto, ON M5T 2P3

Vander Zalm, William (Bill)
former Premier of B.C./B.C. Family Coaltion Party
"Lilac King of Canada"

3553 Arthur Dr.
Delta, BC V4K 3N2

Vanelli, Gino
rock singer

c/o 15003 Greenleaf St.
Sherman Oaks, CA 91403
U.S.A.

Vanier, Jean
founder of L'Arche, an international federation of communities that creates homes for the intellectually disabled/son of former Governor General

L'Arche
B.P. 35, Trosly-Breuil
60350 Cuise-la-Motte
France

Van Vogt, A.E. (Alfred Elton)
science fiction writer

c/o Richard Curtis
Literary Agency
164 East 64th St.
New York, NY 10021
U.S.A.

Varma, Devendra
expert on the supernatural

1020 Belmont on the Arm
Halifax, NS B3H 1J3

Vasik, Cassandra
country singer

49 Ontario St.
Toronto, ON M5A 2V1

Vastel, Michel
journalist/author

c/o *Le Soleil*
390 St-Vallier est
Quebec, PQ G1K 7J6

Veilleux, Gerard
former CBC President/Senior Visiting Fellow, Canadian Centre for Management Development

c/o CCMD
P.O. Box 420, Stn. A
Ottawa, ON K1N 8V4

Verdon, Ray
President, Nabisco Biscuit Co.

2211 SR–208
Fair Lawn, NJ 07410, U.S.A.

Veterans Against Nuclear Arms (VANA)
Cmdr. Robert W. Cocks, National Chairman

Box 3B8, R.R. #1
Tantallon, NS B0J 3J1

VIA Rail Canada
Terry Ivany, President

P.O. Box 8116, Stn. A
Montreal, PQ H3C 2C9

Vickers, Jon *opera singer*	c/o Metropolitan Opera Co. Lincoln Center Plaza New York, NY 10023 U.S.A.
Vigneault, Gilles *singer/poet/Quebec nationalist*	c/o Nouvelles Editions de l'Arc 839 rue Sherbrooke est, #2 Montreal, PQ H2L 1K6
Victims of Violence Gary Rosenfeldt, President *international victims' coalition*	151 Slater St. Ottawa, ON K1P 5H4
Victoria Times Colonist Colin D. McCullough, Publisher	2621 Douglas St., Victoria, BC V8T 4M2
Victorian Order of Nurses (VON) Donna Roe, Executive Director	5 Blackburn Ave. Ottawa, ON K1N 8A2
VISA Canada Association Roger Woodward, President *credit card association*	Scotia Plaza, Ste. 3710 40 King Street W. Toronto, ON M5H 3Y2
Vision TV: Canada's Faith Network Ron Keast, President	315 Queen St. E. Toronto, ON M5A 1S7
***Voir* magazine** Jean Barbe, Editor-in-Chief	4130 rue St. Denis Montreal, PQ H2W 2M5
Voisine, Roch *rock singer*	1665 Victoria, #801-PH2 St. Lambert, PQ J4R 2T6
Volkswagen Canada Clive B. Warrilow, President	1940 Eglinton Ave. E. Scarborough, ON M1L 2M2
Volvo Canada Ltd. Ronny C. Persson, President and CEO	175 Gordon Baker Rd. North York, ON M2H 2N7
Voyageur-Colonial Ltd. Don Haire, President	505 de Maisonneuve est Montreal, PQ H2L 1Y4

W

"The letter which merely answers another letter is no letter at all."

Mark Van Doren

Waldo, Carolyn
Olympic synchronized swimmer

c/o CJOH TV
1500 Merivale Rd.
Ottawa, ON K2E 6Z5

Walker, George F.
playwright

c/o Great North Artists Mgmt.
350 Dupont St.
Toronto, ON M5R 1V9

Walker, Larry
highest-paid Canadian baseball player

c/o Montreal Expos
4549 Pierre de Coubertin
Montreal, PQ H1V 3N7

Wallin, Pamela
co-anchor, CBC's "Prime Time News"

c/o CBC–Prime Time News
P.O. Box 14000, Stn. A
Toronto, ON M5W 1A0

Waltons
rock group

c/o The Agency
41 Britain St., Ste 200
Toronto, ON M5A 1R7

The War Amputations of Canada
Cliff Chadderton, CEO

2827 Riverside Dr.
Ottawa, ON K1V 0C4

Ward, J. Kingsley
businessman and author of *Letters of a Businessman to His Son* and *Letters of a Businessman to His Daughter*

c/o The Vimy Ridge Group
140 Renfrew Dr., #205
Markham, ON L3R 6B3

Ward, Max
former owner of Wardair

69 Westbrook Dr. N.W.
Edmonton, AB T6J 2C8

Watier, Lise
President, Lise Watier Cosmetics
5800 Côte de Liesse
Montreal, PQ H4T 1B4

Watkins, Mel
political scientist/Editor, *This Magazine*
31 Sussex Ave.
Toronto, ON M5S 1J6

Watson, Patrick
journalist/filmmaker,
Chairman, CBC
P.O. Box 8478
Ottawa, ON K1G 3J5

Watt, Charlie
Liberal Senator from Quebec
Room 905-VB
The Senate
Ottawa, ON K1A 0A4

Waxman, Al
actor/director/producer
Chairman, Academy of Canadian Cinema and Television
87 Forest Hill Rd.
Toronto, ON M4V 2L6

Weber, George
Secretary General,
International Federation of Red Cross and Red Crescent Societies
P.O. Box 372
CH-1211 Geneva 19
Switzerland

Webster, Jack
journalist/"Front Page Challenge" *panellist*
c/o CBC–Front Page Challenge
P.O. Box 500, Stn. A
Toronto, ON M5W 1E6

Weigand, William
Mayor of Whitehorse
2121 Second Ave.
Whitehorse, YK Y1A 1C2

Weinzweig, John
composer
107 Manor Rd. E.
Toronto, ON M4S 1R3

Welcome Wagon Ltd.
Pauline Hill, Chairman of the Board/co-owner
3761 Victoria Park Ave.
Unit 10
Agincourt, ON M1W 3S3

Wells, Clyde Kirby
Premier of Newfoundland
Confederation Building, 8th fl.
St. John's, NF A1B 4J6

Wendy's Restaurants of Canada Inc.
Douglas H.W. Gould, President
6715 Airport Rd., Ste. 301
Mississauga, ON L4V 1X2

West Baffin Eskimo Co-operative
T.P. Ryan, Manager
promotes and assists Inuit artists
Cape Dorset, NT X0A 0C0

West Edmonton Mall
Canada's largest shopping mall
8770 170 St. N.W.
Edmonton, AB T5T 3J7

Westell, Anthony
journalist
School of Journalism
Carleton University
Colonel By Dr.
Ottawa, ON K1S 5B6

Western Canada Concept Party
Douglas Christie, founder/Leader
810 Courtney St.
Victoria, BC V8W 1C4

Western Canada Wilderness Committee
Paul George, Executive Director
environmental action group
20 Water Street
Vancouver, BC V6B 1A4

Weston, W. Galen
Chairman and President,
George Weston Ltd.
22 St. Clair Ave. E.
Ste. 2001
Toronto, ON M4T 2S3

Wheeler, Anne
film director/producer
R.R. #1, 212 Sunset Dr.
Ganges, BC V0S 1E0

Whelan, Eugene
former federal Liberal Cabinet Minister from Ontario
self-proclaimed best-recognized former Agriculture Minister in the world
727 Front Rd. N.
Amherstberg, ON N9V 2V6

The Whig-Standard
Gordon Fisher, Publisher
Canada's oldest daily newspaper
306 King St.
Kingston, ON K7L 4Z7

Whitehead, John
calligrapher of the Proclamation of the Constitution and Master Calligrapher to the Government of Canada
27 River Oaks Court
Stittsville, ON K2S 1L3

Whooping Crane Conservation Association
Lorne Scott, Co-ordinator
P.O. Box 995
Indian Head, SK S0G 2K0

Wiarton Willy
Canada's national groundhog
c/o Bill Walker
BIA Co-ordinator
P.O. Box 310
Wiarton, ON N0H 2T0

WIC (Western International Communications Ltd.) Doug Holtby, President and CEO *Canada's largest private broadcaster*	1960 505 Burrard St. Vancouver, BC V7X 1M6
Wicks, Ben *cartoonist*	449-A Jarvis St. Toronto, ON M4Y 2H2
Wiggins, Chris *actor/writer*	c/o First Artists Mgmt. 1255 Yonge St., #303 Toronto, ON M4T 1W6
Wilcox, David *rock singer*	c/o The Agency 41 Britain St., Ste. 200 Toronto, ON M5A 1R7
Wildlife Habitat Canada David J. Neave, Executive Director	1704 Carling Ave. Ottawa, ON K2A 1C7
Wilfrid Laurier University Lorna Marsden, President	Waterloo, ON N2L 3C5
Williams, Brian CBC sports broadcaster	c/o CBC Sports P.O. Box 500, Stn. A Toronto, ON M5W 1E6
Williams, Dave "Tiger" *former hockey player* Vice President, Vancouver Voodoo roller hockey club	c/o Vancouver Voodoo 1200 Lynn Valley Rd. Ste. 302 North Vancouver, BC V7J 2A2
Williams, Lynn President, United Steel Workers of America	5 Gateway Center Pittsburg, PA 15222 U.S.A.
Williams, Richard *animator,* "The Pink Panther" *and* "Roger Rabbit"	c/o 3193 Cahuenga Blvd. West Hollywood, CA 90068 U.S.A.
Wilson, Bertha *first woman justice of the Supreme Court of Canada*	147 Rideau Terrace Ottawa, ON K1M 0Z4
Wilson, Very Rev. Lois M. *former and first woman Moderator, United Church of Canada*	482 Markham St. Toronto, ON M6G 2L3

Wilson, Michael former federal Conservative Cabinet Minister from Ontario	c/o Amoco, Board of Directors 200 E. Randolph Dr. Chicago, IL 60601, U.S.A.
Wilson, Nancy "CBC Newsworld" *journalist*	c/o CBC Newsworld P.O. Box 2640 Calgary, AB T2M 2M7
Windsor Star James Thomson, Publisher	167 Ferry St. Windsor, ON N9A 4M5
Winsor, Hugh National Political Editor, *The Globe and Mail*	165 Sparks St. Ottawa, ON K1P 5B9
Winnipeg Blue Bombers Football Club Cal Murphy, General Manager	1465 Maroons Rd. Winnipeg, MB R3G 0L6
Winnipeg Commodity Exchange Robert P. Purvis, President	500 Commodity Exchange Tower 360 Main St Winnipeg, MB R3C 3Z4
Winnipeg Free Press Maurice H. Switzer, Publisher	1355 Mountain Ave. Winnipeg, MB R2X 3B6
Winnipeg Jets Hockey Club Mike Smith, General Manager	Winnipeg Arena 15–1430 Maroons Rd. Winnipeg, MB R3G 0L5
Winston, Helen *actress*	14233 Valerio St. Van Nuys, CA 91405, U.S.A.
Winterlude/Bal de Neige Suzie Lamothe, Chief *home of the world's largest skating rink*	National Capital Commission 161 Laurier Ave. W. Ottawa, ON K1P 6J6
Withers, Gen. Ramsey Muir former Chief of Defence Staff	c/o Government Consultants International 50 O'Connor St. Ottawa, ON K1P 6L2
Women Who Love Too Much Beverley Hurlburt *self-help group*	c/o Catholic Family Services #102, 1013 Wilson Ave. Downsview, ON M3K 1G1
Women's Legal Education and Action Fund (LEAF) *community legal defence group*	489 College St. Toronto, ON M6G 1A5

Wood, Dalia
Liberal Senator from Quebec

Room 457-S
The Senate
Ottawa, ON K1A 0A4

Wood, Sharon
first North American woman to reach the summit of Mount Everest

P.O. Box 1482
Canmore, AB T0L 0M0

Woodcock, George
author/historian

6429 McCleery St.
Vancouver, BC V6N 1G5

World Championship Bathtub Race
Bill McGuire, Commodore
world's first annual bathtub race

P.O. Box 565
Nanaimo, BC V9R 5L5

World Council of Indigenous Peoples
Donald Rojas, President

555 King Edward Ave.
Ottawa, ON K1N 6N5

World Federalists of Canada
Fergus Watt, Executive Director

#207, 145 Spruce St.
Ottawa, ON K1R 6P1

World Sikh Organization
R.R.S. Chahal, President

P.O. Box 15830
Merivale Depot
Nepean, ON K2C 3S7

World Wildlife Fund Canada
Monte Hummel, President

504, 90 Eglinton Ave. E.
Toronto, ON M4P 2Z7

Worsley, Lorne "Gump"
former hockey goalie

421 rue Bonair
Beloeil, PQ J3G 2B2

Wright, Deborah
first NHL woman scout (1993)

c/o San Jose Sharks
10 Almaden, Ste. 600
San Jose, CA 95113
U.S.A.

Wright, Eric
author

65 Gormley Ave.
Toronto, ON M4V 1T9

Wright, L.R.
mystery writer

11744 Fraserview St.
Maple Ridge, BC V2X 8A8

Wright, Michelle
country singer

c/o Savannah Music Group
1207–17th Ave. S., Ste. 305
Nashville, TN 37212, U.S.A.

Wright, Ronald
travel writer/author

R.R. #1
Campbellcroft, ON L0A 1B0

X

"A letter always feels to me like
Immortality because it is the mind
alone, without corporeal friend.
Indebted in our talk to attitude and accents,
there seems a spectral power
in thought that walks alone."

Emily Dickinson

Xerox Canada Inc.
Diane McGarry, President

5650 Yonge St.
North York, ON M2M 4G7

Y

"Let a letter expect the messenger,
not the messenger the letter."

Torriano

Yalden, Max
Chief Commissioner, Canadian Human Rights Commission
320 Queen St., 13th fl.
Place de Ville, Tower A
Ottawa, ON K1A 1E1

Yamaha Motor Canada Ltd.
Yukio Saguchi, President
480 Gordon Baker Rd.
North York, ON M2H 3B4

Yanovsky, Zal
co-founder, The Lovin' Spoonful rock group
c/o Chez Piggy
68-R Princess St.
Kingston, ON K7L 1A5

Yeo, Leslie James
actor/writer/producer/director
19 Binscarth Rd.
Toronto, ON M4W 1Y2

YMCA Canada (Young Men's Christian Association)
Saul Kasimer, CEO
2160 Yonge St.
Toronto, ON M4S 2A9

Yogen-Fruz International Ltd.
Michael Serruya, co-founder and President
international frozen yogurt franchise
7500 Woodbine Ave.
Markham, ON L3R 1A8

York University
Susan Mann, President
4700 Keele St.
North York, ON M3J 1P3

Yost, Elwy
host, "Saturday Night at the Movies"
6237 St. Georges Cres.
West Vancouver, BC V7W 1Z3

Young, Douglas
federal Liberal Cabinet Minister from New Brunswick/former provincial Party Leader

Room 707–CB
House of Commons
Ottawa, ON K1A 0A6

Young, Neil
rock musician

506 Santa Monica Blvd.
Santa Monica, CA 90401
U.S.A.

Young, Scott
author

1 Middleton Dr.
Peterborough, ON K9J 4Z1

YTV Canada Inc.
youth channel

64 Jefferson Ave., #18
Toronto, ON M6K 3H3

YWCA Canada (Young Women's Christian Association)
Judith Wiley, CEO

80 Gerrard St. E.
Toronto, ON M5B 1G6

Yzerman, Steve
hockey player

c/o Detroit Red Wings
600 Civic Center Dr.
Detroit, MI 48226
U.S.A.

Z

"An intention to write never turns into a letter."

Rainer Maria Rilke

Zapata Design Associates
(Karen Gable and Nancy Young)
fashion designers
1290 Bay St.
Toronto, ON M5R 2C3

Zappacosta, Alfie
rock singer
c/o Lou Blair Management
68 Water St., Ste. 407
Vancouver, BC V6B 1A

Zeidler, Eberhard
architect, Toronto's Eaton Centre and Vancouver's Canada Place
315 Queen St. W.
Toronto, ON M5V 2X2

Zeller's Inc.
Paul Walters, President
department store chain
5100 de Maisonneuve W.
Montreal, PQ H4A 1Y6

Zero Population Growth of Canada
John Meyer, President
P.O. Box 113
Ajax, ON L1S 3C5

Znaimer, Moses
broadcaster/President and Executive Producer, Citytv
c/o Citytv
299 Queen St. W.
Toronto, ON M5V 2Z5

Zolf, Larry
journalist/writer/broadcaster
217 Lippincott St.
Toronto, ON M5S 2P4

Zuckerman, Mortimer B.
U.S. magazine and newspaper publisher/real estate developer
c/o Boston Properties
599 Lexington Ave.
New York, NY 10022-60300
U.S.A.

Zundel, Ernst
anti-Holocaust proponent
206 Carlton St.
Toronto, ON M5A 2L1

Subject Index

JOURNALISM

JUDICICIARY

LABOUR

LANGUAGE/LINGUISTICS

LITERATURE

NATIVE CANADIANS/ORGANIZATIONS

NOBEL PRIZE WINNERS

ORGANIZATIONS (Various)

OTHER

PEACE AND WAR

PHOTOGRAPHY

PLACES/CANADIAN LANDMARKS

POLICE FORCES

POLITICS

POLLSTERS/POLLING FIRMS

PUBLISHERS

RELIGION

SCIENCE

SENATORS

TECHNOLOGY & TELECOMMUNICATIONS

TELEVISION & RADIO

THINK TANKS

UTILITIES

WOMEN'S ACTIVISTS